Welcome
to Wyoming

Welcome to Wyoming

by Christina Wray

*
WordsWorth Publishing
Cody, Wyoming

I would like to thank the families in this book for taking me into their homes and accepting me as one of their own. I recognize that their memories of the events described in this book are different than my own. This memoir is the story of my life. It is not my intention to hurt anyone. Both my publisher and I regret any unintentional harm resulting from the publishing and marketing of this book.

ISBN 978-1-7334897-8-2
First edition paperback

Editor: Renée C. Tafoya
Cover: *North Fork Sentinel*, oil on canvas, © Russell Hamilton
Author photo: © Jonathan A. Meyers

WordsWorth Publishing
Cody, Wyoming
www.wordsworthpublishing.com

For my husband, Greg, who helped me return to
the cabin on Green Creek and the Wapiti Valley
where I belong.

*There are places I'll remember all my life, though some
have changed. Some forever, not for better, some have
gone and some remain. Though I know I'll never loose
affection for people and things that went before, I know
I'll often stop and think about them. In my life, I've
loved you more.*

— John Lennon and Paul McCartney

PROLOGUE

It is my first winter in the cabin on Green Creek. The old timers tell me it will be the worst winter in many years. *Of course, because I am here now.* Will she do what she says she is going to do? Will she stay? Give her a hard winter and she'll leave, move back to New Mexico, shake her head, and tell people it was too hard. Twenty-below for weeks at a time. Three feet of snow outside the door. Forty-mile-an-hour winds ripping at the cabin roof. My own private herd of deer eating the corn I bought at Cody Feed. Coyotes howling and yipping, surrounding the cabin. Cracks in the cabin walls letting in the cold. Thawing out frozen pipes with a hair dryer. The fireplace insert cranking out the only heat. Chopping wood, carrying wood, splitting wood, cutting down dead trees—a constant challenge for my husband, who grew up in Maine, so he knows about winter, he says, but who just last week stood in the doorway of the bedroom and, with some desperation, said, "Make it stop snowing! Please!"

Winter depresses me. The snow-covered mountains are cold and rigid. Darkness comes too early and stays too late. My room is cold. I bought a radiant heater at Walmart. Dressing to take the dogs out to pee takes fifteen minutes of putting on layers: long johns, cotton turtleneck, heavy sweater, wool pants, snow boots, and wool gloves. All this for ten minutes of breathing frigid air through my black ski mask purchased on Amazon, which makes me look like I'm going to rob the nearest convenience store. Once back inside the cabin, all the heavy clothes have to be peeled off. The fire needs tending. The wood pellet stove in the back room needs to be stoked. I spend the entire winter sweeping up ashes, cleaning out ashes, dumping ashes, and starting a new pile of ashes. I wipe ashes from the log beams. I am pretty sure I breathe in some of the ashes.

In the wintertime, I eat like a bear preparing for hibernation. I gain five pounds in the first month. None of my jeans fit, so I order bigger jeans on the Internet. I wear baggy sweatpants and floppy slippers. Out of pure boredom, I make cookies. Oatmeal raisin and chocolate chip. I gain five more pounds and start wearing my flannel Disneyland pajamas all the time. My depression deepens. I start looking for low-fare airline tickets to Del Mar or San Diego. Anywhere but here.

And then I woke up one dark winter morning and remembered the reason I moved back to my cabin on Green Creek. It was hard to transform my life from a busy workaholic living in a dirty city full of crime, with everyone there rushing, hurrying, worrying. Hard to give up the steady income and the frantic scrabbling for position. Annoyed most of the time, constantly afraid that I would be carjacked, abducted, robbed, or worse.

That is gone now. I feel as though I have been released from prison, paroled on the North Fork of the Shoshone River, the valley where I grew up so many years ago. The phone seldom rings. I forget to check my email. Cell phones don't work here. My only real problem seems to be where I put my glasses.

I quit my job of twenty-five years and moved back to Wyoming. I tell people I'm retired.

Friends ask me what I'm going to do up there in the mountains. I was raised by a pack of writers, mostly women, though my biological father was a journalist who wrote feature stories for the *Boston Herald*. My mother owned a small-town newspaper in Amesbury, Massachusetts, which was just over the border from our New Hampshire farm. She wrote editorials as well as feature articles. My grandmother wrote children's stories and published many of them. My aunt majored in English literature in college and wrote articles in her profession as an occupational therapist. My mother started me out writing at an early age. Instead of saying "Go watch TV" as most parents do now, she would say, "Go write me a story." The world could be coming to an end, and we would all be arguing about how to write about it. Any major event in our lives was just considered good story material. With this background, I have no choice but to write. It's out of my hands. Now I have no excuses. I have been dreaming of living at the cabin for many years. Sitting in front of the fire looking out over the valley, forming thoughts that don't include making a living or dealing with angry people who have no dreams. All this and the peace of knowing I have done the right thing. I have come back to my roots. I will die in Wyoming. I don't know of a better place to spend eternity.

WELCOME TO WYOMING

In 1959, my mother had what today would be considered a midlife crisis. She announced to her stunned family that she had accepted a teaching position in a one-room schoolhouse located in Wapiti, Wyoming. My grandmother had one of her spells and took to her bed for a week. My seventeen-year-old sister cried because she had a new boyfriend, and she didn't want to leave him. I had mixed feelings about going to Wyoming. The lure of cowboys and horses was almost more intriguing than being with my grandmother. And my mother said we would return to New England after her year of teaching was completed. As a widowed schoolteacher, she wanted to see if she could make it on her own in the West. Also, I believe she had just read Owen Wister's *The Virginian*. In July of 1959, we left Boston for Wyoming in what might have been a covered wagon, though with gasoline and other modern conveniences such as toilets and restaurants, on a journey that changed the course of our lives.

We loaded up our 1956 two-tone green Chevy station wagon with a small open utility trailer attached, hauling our possessions as well as camping equipment. My mother very bravely set off with two fighting daughters and two restless dogs in a car with no air conditioning during the hottest part of the summer. My mother thought it would be fun to camp out along the way, but we soon found, due to a sad lack of campgrounds and the scorching July heat, that we stayed in motels more than expected. Always the educator, my mother wanted to prolong the trip and make it a learning experience for us. We drove up through Maine and into Canada, then over to the Great Lakes. We went through the Sioux St. Marie locks on a ferry and drove down through North and South Dakota. We saw Mt. Rushmore as well as the Mitchell Corn Palace. I admired my mother's courage in negotiating roads such as the Shell Canyon Highway in the Big Horn Mountains just west of Sheridan, Wyoming. For a flatlander afraid of heights, she did quite well, even when faced with the "Dam Hill" west of Cody, Wyoming. This was a famous twisting mass of tunnels drilled through solid granite with steep 11% grades. There was a one-lane road through most of the canyon, and several times we had to back up to allow larger vehicles to pass. At the bottom of the Dam Hill there was a man with a tractor who, for a certain amount of money, would tow tourists up the hill. My mother rolled down her window, talked to the man for a few minutes, then set her jaw and said she could make it on her own, thank you very much. It was a steering-wheel-gripper, and she broke out in a sweat near the top, but we made it.

With the Dam Hill and the Shoshone Canyon

negotiated, we burst into the Wapiti Valley west of Cody. Rugged 12,000-foot mountains surrounded acres of lush alfalfa fields, sandstone formations, and sage-covered hills. We wound our way through the valley, speechless at the beauty of the landscape which was to be our new home. We saw huge log ranch houses built by real Wyoming ranchers. We saw horses, cattle, and sheep. We arrived at Wapiti School around midday. The log schoolhouse had a two-room teacherage where we were to live. The school itself consisted of a foyer with a single bathroom, a large room filled with desks and chalkboards, and a small room off the main one, which served as an office for my mother as well as a library filled with secondhand books. We unloaded the station wagon and settled in. The head of the school board drove up in a battered Ford pickup truck. We stared at his cowboy hat, boots, and his large silver belt buckle. "Welcome to Wyoming," he said.

When school began at Wapiti that first year, many new experiences opened for me. There were eight grades and twelve children. I was in the fourth grade with a girl named Karen Krone, my sole classmate. Karen had an older sister and two younger brothers who also attended Wapiti School. Karen's father was the Forest Ranger in the Shoshone National Forest. They lived about ten miles west of the school in the oldest ranger station in North America. Karen and I became close friends, and I spent a lot of time with her at the old log cabin ranger station where we fished, camped, and hiked. We read every Western novel we could get our hands on — Zane Grey, Owen Wister, Louis L'Amour. We learned how to build a small campfire under a juniper bush so the smoke would dissipate through the branches, and we wouldn't be seen by passing marauders. We wore Levi's and cowboy boots. We stole a pack of Camel cigarettes from her father and made ourselves sick smoking out behind the horse barn. We both agreed that we were born in the wrong time. We longed for the early 1800s with stagecoaches and horse-drawn wagons.

In those days, there was no Child Safety Act to protect us from playground equipment. The playground was covered with gravel, cactus, and sagebrush. There was an antiquated swing set with a rusty chain link holding up a splintery wooden seat. There was a wooden teeter-totter, a rickety metal slide, and a tetherball pole with a rope, but no ball attached. There was a strange-looking round wooden contraption with metal bars riveted into the wood in a wedge-shaped pattern. The object was to grab the metal handles and run around and around until the wooden spool was going fast, and then jump on and hang on for dear life. The smaller children usually missed the jumping-on part and were dragged around in the dirt until their knees were bloody. Those of us who jumped on successfully ended up appropriately nauseated and dizzy. Most of us spent the entire school year picking gravel out of abrasions on our knees and elbows.

The small community of Wapiti consisted mostly of ranchers, farmers, dude ranches, and outfitters. Our closest neighbors were George and Inez King, who ran the Wapiti Post Office in a small log-sided addition connected to Wapiti Lodge, which they also owned and operated. There were a few rustic cabins for tourists. Inez ran the dining room, cooking breakfast and dinner for summer guests. The schoolhouse was the focal point of the valley where meetings were held, voting took place, and carry-in potluck suppers occurred on Saturday nights. All the food was homemade by some of the best cooks in the valley. The food tables were filled with chocolate cakes, apple pies, baked beans and potato salad, chicken casseroles, freshly baked cinnamon rolls, brownies, sheet cakes, and fried chicken. To this day, I remember the taste of Ethel Montgomery's famous mince pie and Mary Ballinger's homemade dinner rolls.

After supper on Saturday nights, the floor was cleared, and the square dancing began. There were four or five local men who played various instruments: Jim Montgomery on guitar, Don Legg on harmonica, Larry Krone on banjo, and Hank Halavichek on the fiddle, as well as acting as the caller for square dancing. The men would sit in a circle drinking coffee, smoking, tuning up, and talking about what music to play. They knew a lot of old-style western waltzes and two-steps.

Drinking alcohol was not allowed, although several of the men would disappear periodically and return smelling of whiskey. The dancing and eating continued long after midnight. The smaller, sleepy children were wrapped in quilts and tucked away under the food tables.

The schoolhouse was not the only place valley residents gathered. People took turns having "musicals" at each other's houses. The scenario was about the same, but there was no dancing, only eating and listening to the men playing their tunes. The women spent most of their time in the kitchen preparing food and gossiping. The children played cards and board games and eavesdropped on the gossip. There were barn dances at several of the local ranchers' horse barns, which included square dancing and eating, and gossiping.

The camaraderie of the Saturday night suppers and dancing is a thing of the past now. The population of the valley has tripled or quadrupled. Most of the ranchland has been sold off and subdivided. When I moved back to the valley in 2007, I was appalled at the magnitude of the growth. Expensive log houses dot the landscape, with a new one popping up almost monthly. I have gotten to know some of my close neighbors on Green Creek, but as for the rest of the valley, I have no idea who they are or where they came from. The one good thing that remains is Wapiti School. It has undergone remodeling from time to time, adding a gymnasium and more classrooms. Instead of grades one through eight, it now offers kindergarten through fifth grade only. There are four teachers, and the playground is now a grassy lawn with more kid-friendly apparatuses to play on. Whenever I drive by Wapiti School on my way to town, I always look back fondly on my time there.

The move to Wyoming and a new school was not difficult for me, but I did miss my Sprague School friends. Especially Peggy McMahon, who was my best friend. When we started kindergarten together, I had trouble adjusting. Separation anxiety and fear of strangers were more than I could deal with, and I cried every day. My mother was teaching first grade in the very next classroom, so Miss Stone, my teacher, took me by the hand and led me across the hall to see my mother. She opened the door and said, "Tina, your mother is right there. OK?" My mother came over and told me everything was all right, just go back to your room. When we came back into the kindergarten room, Peggy was there and took me by the hand. She talked to me and told me she had been scared to come to school, but everything was working out. She was more gregarious than I was with the other kids. She also lived right across the street from the school. Every day at noon, we walked across the street to Peggy's house and had cream cheese and grape jelly sandwiches. Her mother, Lucille, became good friends with my mother. Peggy was allowed to come visit me at the farm on some weekends. When we moved to Wyoming, Peggy came to visit the ranch when we were both in sixth grade. We explored the ranch together. We rode horses and herded sheep. We walked to a spot by the river where we found fossils. She took a fossil home with her and still has that fossil to this day.

Peggy and I have kept in touch over the years, although during our marriages and her childbearing years, we were busy and didn't write often. She was always there, however, in the back of my mind. When Greg and I moved to Wyoming in 2007, Peggy and I started corresponding again. She and Jack came out to visit us a few times. I flew back to her Connecticut house outside of Granby and stayed for a few days. We went to a Red Sox game. We reunited with one of our kindergarten friends, Tommy Hodgsen, who keeps in touch through Facebook.

Peggy's three children are now grown and out on their own. Peggy and Jack are retired, and they spend a lot of time traveling to see their kids. We send each other books and email occasionally. I will always remember her kindness toward me when I was vulnerable.

VIRGINIA

Virginia Belle Evans was born on October 26, 1914, in the south bedroom of the farmhouse in South Hampton, New Hampshire. Five years later, her sister, Shirley Eliza Evans, was born in the same south bedroom of the farmhouse. Virginia attended a small, one-room schoolhouse about a mile down the road from the farm. Her grandfather, Charles Morrill Evans, owned hundreds of acres and was a successful dairy farmer, as well as serving as County Selectman for many years. Virginia's father, Willis J. Evans, worked the farm with his father. Her mother, Isabelle Currier Swain Evans, ran the household and established a nursing home next door to the farm, which she called Fitz Memorial Home.

Virginia attended high school in Amesbury, Massachusetts, just across the border from South Hampton. After high school, she attended Boston University and graduated with honors with a degree in journalism. While attending BU, she met Frederick John Rae, also a journalism major. They were married at the South Hampton farm on July 16, 1938. They lived in Cambridge for a few years. Fred worked as a reporter and feature writer for the *Boston Herald*. My mother wrote a column for the *Herald*. My sister, Candace Shannon Rae, was born in 1941, after which Fred and Virginia moved to the farm and lived with Isabelle and Willis. Fred and Virginia bought the small-town Amesbury newspaper and worked there together. Fred continued to write for the *Boston Herald*, commuting to Boston five days a week on the train.

Fred was diagnosed with a glioblastoma, a malignant, inoperable brain tumor. He continued to write for the *Herald* until his death in May 1951. Willis died in 1952. Virginia and Isabelle sold Fitts Memorial and bought a house in West Newton, Massachusetts, so that my mother could go back to school, and Isabelle could take care of her two granddaughters. My mother obtained a master's degree in education from BU. She took a job teaching first grade at Sprague Elementary School in Wellesley. On weekends, we would load up the car and drive to the South Hampton farm where we spent many wonderful summers.

My mother was an excellent teacher. Outside the classroom, however, Virginia was opinionated and argumentative. She rubbed people the wrong way. She was always embroiled in some sort of fight with neighbors, merchants, employers, or family members. Virginia also held the title of Queen of the Nasty Letter. I often regret that she died when she did because with the Internet and email, she could have fired off her letters and blogs instantly. As it was, she tapped out her correspondence on an old Royal typewriter with a broken letter E.

My mother's decision to travel to Wyoming was not only made as a mid-life crisis, but was an attempt to get away from her mother and sister. Virginia argued constantly with them. My grandmother, though a very intelligent and literary person, was a champion worrier. At any given moment, she could come up with the most horrendous thing that could happen to any one of us. Hence, my mother, my sister, and my Aunt Shirley were the worst "awfulizers" imaginable, as well as being tremendous hypochondriacs. Part of the reason behind leaving Boston for Wyoming was to save me from this terrible fate.

Aunt Shirley told me that on the day we loaded up the station wagon and left for Wyoming, my grandmother sank to her knees, wailing and sobbing. Shirley had to help her up and guide her back into the house. Granny told Shirley that she would never see us again, and that was exactly what happened. She died of a broken heart several years later. I never saw my grandmother again.

My mother was a critical woman. She hounded my sister Candy, picked on her, and called her things like "you stupid idiot" right in front of us. It was inconceivable to Virginia that she could have a daughter who was not bright. Candy was not a good student and was not considered to be "college material." Virginia put all her money on me. I was pushed and told I had to accomplish something in my life. "You have an I.Q. of 120 for God's sake. Use it!" I must have heard this 100 times during my childhood, which made me intentionally underachieve, a practice which I continue to this day.

Virginia was helpful and patient with people outside the family. She taught school at Wapiti and in Cody for many years and ended up starting the Head Start Program in Powell, which is still going strong today. But with her own children, she was impatient. We both grew up thinking that *goddamnittohell* (my mother's favorite epithet) was all one word. Candy has never forgiven her. I, on the other hand, was able to rise above it all and find some semblance of happiness, though I don't know quite how I did that. Four years of psychotherapy helped. After my mother died, I felt released and relieved. No more critical disapproving lectures about wasting my life. Candy was not so lucky. She told me once, years ago, that she only stayed with her first husband, Bob, who was at least a psychopath, because she didn't want to admit she was wrong in marrying him, and that our mother was *right*. Thus, she lived with a crazy man for 25 years and had a crazy daughter who died of an overdose of Percocet at age forty. With all her faults, however, my mother tried her best to educate me and my sister. She exposed us to the arts, literature, and music. I remember the ballet in Boston, the Museum of Art, the Aquarium, various classical music concerts, and High Tea at one of the fancy hotels in Boston. She took me to a nightclub once to see Burl Ives where I had a "pink lady" and sat right in front of the stage.

I sucked it all in, and it stuck with me. I remember every detail of my life from around age five. Candy, on the other hand, does not remember much of anything. She has blocked out a lot of her life, and when prodded into trying to remember, she will burst into tears and say she doesn't know.

My grandmother had a saying which I still use today. She would ask us what possessed us to do something. What possessed you to break that vase? What possessed you to tell me a lie? I can still hear her saying what possessed Virginia to move us to Wyoming. Most of us in the family wondered that, but only my grandmother said it out loud.

The following article appeared in the *Christian Science Monitor*, January 1960. I had been struggling with writing this Wyoming memoir for some time when my computer went down, and I paced around the cabin, waiting for it to be fixed. During one of these pacing episodes, I decided to clean out the storage shed at the back of the property. In an old trunk marked "Evans Family," I discovered a tattered photo album that had newspaper articles glued to the back of the black construction paper pages. I had never read this article. Apparently, my mother sent it to Aunt Shirley, who was the family gatekeeper of treasured memories. Stranger still, the name "Tina" is written in my mother's handwriting at the top of the newspaper article. After reading this article, I knew I had to include it in my book. The answer to the question "What possessed you to move to Wyoming?" is answered in more detail.

MY ONE-ROOM SCHOOL IN THE VALLEY
By Virginia Rae

I don't really know when I first thought of going West to teach in a one-room, eight-grade school, but one day in February, when most of the teachers despair of making it through to the end of the year, I sat down and wrote to boards of education in Montana, Colorado, and Wyoming. My letter said, "I am tired of my plush-lined rut. I want to teach in a country school where there are no supervisors, no interruptions, just a chance to teach; and I hope to find children who are not spoiled by too much of everything, who want to learn.

It goes without saying that the boards were a bit skeptical of my good intentions and of my willingness to take a $2000 drop in salary in order to teach eight grades in a country school, but the need for rural teachers is so great — Montana, for instance, has 40 vacancies for every teacher applying — that they sent me things to fill out and requested a recent photo. Some literature also arrived from the chambers of commerce.

The Dude Ranchers Association brochure, which was included, set me to dreaming. I wrote to some of the ranchers and asked if there was any possibility of living near a ranch while teaching. Among the replies, one from Wapiti, Wyoming, sounded good. "Our teacher, having been here for eight years, is leaving for greener pastures. There is a vacancy in our little school by the river." Although later I had literally dozens of offers in three states, I settled on Wapiti because of its location 25 miles from Yellowstone National Park.

I don't suppose I shall ever feel well-prepared in all subjects for all grades, but fortunately the modern textbooks make teaching fairly foolproof.

The Saturday before school began, all the

parents and some of the neighbors came for a clean-up morning, bringing a potluck lunch. Everybody had a good time and the school was thoroughly cleaned, windows and all. It was amusing to see the men in their blue jeans, cowboy boots and big hats, looking for all the world like cowboys in a Western movie, fixing swings and teeter- totters and mending the slide.

At noon, everybody sat on the cement-floored porch and ate baked beans, salad and frankfurters, while the eternal sun poured down.

"D-Day" arrived all too soon. My stomach was in its usual first-day-of-school state as I awaited the two private cars which would bring my 12 children. Both cars arrived at once and the children filed in, quietly and politely.

There were six boys and six girls. The little first grader, Billy Chamberlain, never having been to school before, came in with his cowboy hat on and new cowboy boots thumping on the hall floor. He sat down like a miniature adult, with a careless arm-over-the-back-of-the-chair attitude. I don't think he said a word out loud all day. I soon discovered that these children are well-trained. They read with pleasure and excitement and know how to read reference books.

Whenever a new project in social studies or science comes up, they go immediately to the school library and look up the information they need.

Two months and 3000 miles later, I found myself driving up to the "little schoolhouse by the river" on a hot August morning with my two daughters, ages 9 and 18, and our two dogs. Here we were, meeting the clerk of the school board and his mother in the yard of the log cabin ranch house building that is the school. We stepped inside, and in a moment I learned what a "teacherage" in like. I had toyed with the intriguing term ever since I had begun correspondence with western communities. They nearly all furnish teacherages for their teachers.

Ours is a one-room apartment with an adjoining modern bath. It has a pine-paneled kitchen unit along one wall with an electric stove, refrigerator, and cabinets above and below the sink. A divan and chair convert into beds, so that by day the room is a charming livingroom. It is all furnished except for linens and dishes.

Opposite the teacher's room is the school library, a very well-equipped little room, and the classroom is at the rear of the building. The latest chrome-and-Formica furniture, fluorescent lighting, and a waxed hardwood floor make this room a pleasant and efficient workshop.

This tiny community of ranchers is able to provide an excellent school for its children on a budget of around $10,000 a year. It is true that the teacher is paid under $5000, but she has the teacherage rent-free with all utilities paid; and she has incomparable scenery, eager students, and plenty of weekend leisure.

Our things were soon unpacked and we were left to ourselves. I couldn't stay indoors. The mountains on either side of the highway were blue and inviting and seemed only a few minutes away. The sagebrush-covered slopes were dry and brown, but the irrigated alfalfa fields by the river were a lush green. To us born-and-bred New Englanders used to the closed-in gentle landscapes of the East, this western spaciousness and ruggedness was almost overwhelming.

School began on August 31, so I spent the next two weeks planning work for eight grades in ten subjects. It seemed hopeless to try and acquaint myself with all the subject matter, which ranged from reading readiness to eight grade science. That first day of school was pretty rugged. It began at 6:30 for me and I was still working at 8:30 that evening, with some time out for a breather and some meals. By the end of the week, however, we had evolved a plan which functions quite smoothly. Grades are combined in social studies, English, and science. Often, too, drill in arithmetic is needed by three or four grades and they drill each other with pleasure. In our present study of irrigation and the geology of this area, all grades take part in this project.

The first three grades need the teacher's direction and help in most subjects, but from the fourth grade up, a minimum of direction is needed. Regular instruction periods in key subjects are given to each grade, of course, but they are on their own after that. One of the greatest advantages of a school of this type is that the children are thrown upon their own resources and must think and act for themselves. They know their assignments and what papers are due, and only an occasional reminder is needed.

The school is organized as a club, with a president, vice-president, secretary and treasurer. Any decisions about playground rules, housekeeping jobs, parties, field trips, and projects are made by the group, under parliamentary procedure. Group discipline is excellent.

The weeks fly by. Here in our little oasis of learning we study and watch the mountains and note the snow showers constantly going on up there. Every week the snow creeps closer to our sunny valley, and the mornings are crisp with frost. Each day's work is important, each day's work goes on uninterrupted by the outside world. But we are not out of touch. We discuss Khrushchev's visit with President Eisenhower, juvenile delinquency in New York, and the situation in Laos.

There is a timelessness and peace in our valley that I have not found elsewhere. There is time to pursue a subject to its end; there is time to investigate, to question, to discover. And there is a sense of safety. Whatever may be going on over the rimrock, it hardly touches us here. Yet we are not indifferent to the problems of the world. These children are learning how to be good and intelligent citizens so that they may go out one day and help solve some of those problems.

FRED

In my dreams, I am a little girl, hiding under the round oak kitchen table at the New Hampshire farmhouse. My father is sitting at the table, drinking his morning coffee and reading the newspaper. I tug on his pant leg and peek out at him from under the oilcloth table cover. Hi, Daddy, I say. He looks down at me and smiles. Hi yourself, he says. He puts his newspaper down and reaches for me, lifting me onto his lap. I lean into him, resting my head on his chest. He picks up the paper and begins reading me a story about Penny the Skunk, a piece he has written for his weekly newspaper column. In my dreams, I remember my father holding me and reading me stories. In my waking life, I have no memories of him. He died of a brain tumor when I was a year old.

My father wrote feature stories for the *Boston Herald*. He was a newspaper man, a reporter with a press pass, a felt fedora and a trench coat. He usually had a cigar hanging out of the corner of his mouth. He was a short, mild-mannered man with a quiet demeanor and a wry sense of humor. He loved the family farm in New Hampshire, where he lived with my mother, my grandmother, and my sister. Every weekday morning, my mother would drive him to the train station in Newburyport to catch the commuter train to Boston. Every evening around 7:00, she drove back to the station to pick him up.

All I know about my father is contained in a cardboard box marked "Fred." There are wedding pictures, family pictures, his death certificate, and his press pass. There are aging copies of the *Boston Herald* with feature articles and news stories written by him. There are letters remembering him from relatives who knew him, though they are all dead now as well. There is a long letter written to Candy from his brother, Johnston Wray, in California. My mother was not one to talk about my father. She was angry with him for leaving her with two daughters, a widowed mother, and no money. She was angry with him because he neglected to tell her that he had a brother living in California and a sister living in Worcester, whom she met for the first time at his funeral.

At the same time my father was diagnosed with glioblastoma, he began coverage of the story of a lifetime. Dr. Hermann Sander of Manchester, New Hampshire was accused of killing patients who were dying from cancer by injecting air into the bloodstream. There was a huge trial beginning February 28, 1950, ending with an acquittal on March 10, 1950. My father was there covering the whole drama as it unfolded. My sister mentioned that she remembered being there with my mother. Even though she was only nine years old, she can recall the excitement and tension in the courtroom.

As I read my father's riveting details of the trial, with tears in my eyes I realized that I was there for him (in my mother's womb) at the most important time in his career, just as he was there for me at my birth on April 20, 1950.

My sister and I ponder our lives if he had lived. We would not have moved to Wyoming. We would have stayed on the farm, gone to college, married New England men. In our wishful thinking, our mother would not have died of breast cancer. We would have stayed together as a unit, a family. But we are here now with our lives twisting and turning on different paths. Whenever I see a Red Sox game, I think of him. Would we have gone to baseball games together, eaten hot dogs and peanuts and sat in the rain at Fenway Park, yelling at the pitcher? Would I have learned how to swim? What would he have taught me? I have his face, his wry smile, his sense of humor, and his hypertension. I have his love of writing and his love of nature. I have his eye for a good story. I just want to know, does he see me here now in the place I want to be, happy with my life at last?

Today, I sit at my computer writing, thinking about Fred Wray. I think about the South Hampton farm and the stories he wrote for the *Boston Herald*. Wyoming fits my internal landscape now. I can't imagine living anywhere else. Yet the "What If" part of life is still there in the background, nagging at me. Do we get another chance as all the reincarnation people think? Or is this it, one life, and then blackness? I can't believe that. I know in my heart and soul that there is more waiting for us. I know I will find my father.

THE RIVER

Today is my mother's birthday. October 26th. In her honor, a storm is blowing in from the East. Snow is predicted. Cold weather is finally coming to stay. It is windy and the last of the cottonwood leaves fly past my window.

Candy just emailed me. We reminisce about the good times at the farm in New Hampshire — spreading newspaper on the round oak table so we could have fresh lobster with melted butter for dinner. Taking the train to Boston to see the ballet. Selling fresh corn at Salisbury Beach. My mother was an avid gardener. She planted a quarter acre of corn every spring — Seneca 60 — the sweetest corn in New England. In the fall we sold peaches from our orchard. She always found ways to make extra money so we could go camping in Maine or skiing in Vermont. Most of my happy memories of my mother revolve around the New Hampshire farm, the farm she gave up when she married her Wyoming rancher.

Today, I live in Wapiti, Wyoming at my cabin on Green Creek. The farm is a distant memory. Most of our relatives are dead. My sister Candy and my cousin

Caroline remain. My daughter, Tamy, lives in Salt Lake City, Utah. My sister's daughter, Heather, died of a drug overdose in 2008. My mother died of breast cancer in 1975. My Aunt Shirley died in 2001 after a long struggle with Alzheimer's. Sometimes the losses overwhelm me and sadness overtakes me. At these times, I walk down to the river and sit on a boulder until the sadness passes. The sounds of the water always heal me.

My mother introduced me to the North Fork of the Shoshone River when I was nine. One day she grabbed her fishing pole and announced that we were going to catch a fish for dinner. I followed her down the hill to the river and sat on a boulder, watching her cast. Within ten minutes, she had a fish on the line, and she pulled in a 17-inch rainbow trout. I was so excited I almost fell in the water trying to help her land the fish. We were breathless and exhilarated. We walked back up the hill with the catch, where my mother showed me how to clean the fish. We had baked trout for supper that night. My relationship with the river started on that day and has never ended.

There are bigger rivers, wilder rivers, rivers with more oomph. The Snake, for example, or the Yellowstone, but the North Fork of the Shoshone will always have a place in my heart. Over the years, I learned how to fish and was allowed to go by myself as I got older. I remember the special fishing hole where I caught my first trout. The gravel bar where I hunted for petrified wood. The ford where we drove our cattle across the river in the summers to graze on BLM land. The magic pool where the water is aquamarine and the river talks to those who will listen. I grew up fishing and walking by the river, telling the river my best hopes, crying at the river's edge over some recent emotional trauma, and saying good-bye to the river when I left the valley and went out into the world, away from the places I loved the most.

I was absent from the valley for nearly thirty years. Recently, I retired and moved back to the North Fork, to the cabin on Green Creek, where I announced to whoever would listen that I was home to stay. For years I had been telling my husband about my river. I wanted him to know it the way I did. I wanted him to learn how to listen to the sounds of the river, to respect the river, and to become best friends with the North Fork of the Shoshone.

My husband, Greg, and I came from New Mexico to the cabin on Green Creek in June 2007 with two elderly dogs and a giant U-Haul truck. The move was hot and exhausting and the river was high and muddy with spring runoff. Fishing was out of the question so we cleaned up the property, cut down dead cottonwoods, revived the lawn, organized our belongings, and sat on the porch at the end of the day planning our next projects. Toward the middle of July, the river started to clear up and settle down. On a Friday morning in mid July we had enough of moving in and decided to take a trip up the North Fork for our first fishing day. We drove in silence to a spot I remembered as a good hole. Our mood was unsettled, anxious, and we bickered about small things. We tromped down to the river and stood by the water. I knelt down, dipping my hands and splashing water on my face. Greg whispered "Look!"

We watched as a bald eagle flew up above the river, right over our heads, so close to us we could look him in the eye. He settled in a huge pine tree about 100 yards up river, studying us closely.

Totally calm now, we gathered our gear and set ourselves up to fish. The day was warming up, the sky clear. The odor of hot pine pitch drifted over us. There was no wind. I sat on a boulder and watched as Greg made his first cast. And on this first cast, the river gave up an 18-inch Cutthroat to the New Mexico native. As I watched him land his first Wyoming trout, tears streamed down my face. I was finally reunited with my old Shoshone friend.

That day, we fished all morning, off and on. I caught a couple of nice Rainbows. We had a picnic lunch on a gravel bar and looked for petrified wood. We talked about fishing and leaving New Mexico to move to Wyoming. We skipped stones across the wide, calm places in the river. We drove back to the cabin and Greg cleaned the fish. We had grilled trout for dinner. That evening we sat on the porch and watched the long summer shadows spread out across Jim Mountain. We sat and smoked and opened a bottle of wine. Greg reached out and touched my hand, glancing over at me. We shared a look without speaking, knowing that we had just had the best day fishing and that we both had come home.

I know coming back to the cabin and the valley was right. There is a palpable magic here. It is a magic sustained by all those who came before — thousands of years of reverence for the mountains and the rivers. It is not personal, but it is all-encompassing. We are lucky to be able to feel it and see it. It is a humbling magic, set forth by the lines of the earth and the web of life entwined by it.

Every trip to town is a wondrous experience. How many times I have driven the 24 miles through the canyon, past the lake and up the river into the mountains is a mathematical problem I have long since given up trying to solve. Coming through the canyon, seeing the snow-covered peaks, endless in their height and beauty, brings me to tears. Majesty, splendor, spectacular — all words I use to try and describe what I see, but it is indescribable. The valley is my safe haven. The mountains protect me. There is always the thought in the back of my mind that I could flee to them and survive. The mountains would help me if I asked them, but they would give no quarter. I would be on my own.

THE RANCH

While teaching that first year at Wapiti School, my mother met Don, a local rancher who also drove the school bus. Their friendship soon turned into a romance, and they passed notes to each other in empty egg cartons (Don's mother sold us farm-fresh eggs), which didn't fool any of us kids. We all knew what was going on. Their romance was the talk of the valley. Don was fifteen years younger than Virginia. The gossip spread like wildfire. The general disapproval was palpable, and Don's family did not give their blessing.

My mother married the rancher in June of 1960. I was ten years old. My sister had moved back to the New Hampshire farm after marrying Bob Livermore. Mother had found her "Virginian." Don was a tall, lanky man whom my mother described as looking like Chester on *Gunsmoke*. Their honeymoon consisted of a pack trip up Sweetwater Creek into the Absaroka Mountains. It rained the entire time. The horses escaped on the first night but were returned to them by an outfitter a couple of days later. The creek was high and muddy because of the rain, thus no fishing. The tent leaked and the campfire kept going out, but they persevered. They did come back two days earlier than planned. They had left me, or I should say abandoned me, to the craziness of my new family.

Maude, now my step-grandmother, was kind and friendly. She fed me sugar cookies and pancakes and tried to ease the pain of separation. The rest of the family eyed me as though I were some strange species plopped down in their midst. I cried the entire time my mother was gone. I cried myself to sleep, and I woke up crying. The in-laws tried to comfort me, the grandchildren tried to play with me, and the grandparents wrung their hands and wondered what to do. I don't think they had ever seen such a severe case of separation anxiety. My sister was gone, my mother was gone, and I was alone and scared to death of the odd family with whom I had been dumped.

When my mother returned a week or so later, I was still crying. I was so depressed that I sat on the front steps of the trailer house in which we now lived and cried for hours. My mother was so alarmed she took me to a psychiatrist (let it be known here that any time in our lives when we showed any type of aberrant emotion, we were taken to a psychiatrist). The psychiatrist tried to question me and was met with absolute silence, except for the crying. I couldn't tell him why I was crying. Years later, when she was dying, my mother wrote me an unsettling letter, and mentioned the crying episode when they were on their honeymoon. I think she thought I was jealous of her, going off with Don. Why was it so hard for everyone to see that I felt lost and abandoned? The New England family was far away, my real father dead,

Candy gone, Virginia now gone off with some strange man. I think I was crying for what would happen in the future. I believed things were going to go badly and end in disaster, but I couldn't formulate a reason. I was crying for all of us.

When my mother married into Don's family, it became clear to me that I would not be going back to New England. Virginia chose a new family and a new permanent location. Essentially Wyoming was now my home.

She insisted that Don adopt me so that I would be part of his family as well. This did not sit well with me. I was not consulted about the decision to be adopted and I resented that my name was legally changed. I resented my new name all through grade school and high school, feeling like it was kind of a curse. Don's family were tough, hard-working, people. His parents, Mary and Jim, had eight children — four boys and four girls. Jim ruled the eight children with an iron hand. When my mother and I arrived on the scene in 1959, all the children were grown, and the girls had all married and moved away. The oldest son left the ranch and worked as an engineer in various Wyoming towns. Dororthy, the oldest daughter, never married and was a school teacher most of her life. She returned to the ranch in the summertime to help Mary. By that time, Jim was elderly with severe emphysema and was unable to work on the ranch, although he did offer his unsolicited opinion quite often. Don and his other brothers remained on the main ranch.

My New England family consisted of my grandmother, my Aunt Shirley, my mother, my sister, and me. All the men had died. I was raised in a family of women with no male influences.

Coming to the Wyoming male-dominated ranch was a frightening yet intriguing experience. The Wyoming cowboy was no longer a Zane Gray myth. My classmates at Wapiti School wore Levi's and cowboy boots. Most of the children lived on ranches and had their own horses to ride. My first horse experience came one day when Don and his brother were moving their cows up the highway to a summer pasture. My mother was riding along as well. Don had a huge dapple-gray Quarter-Horse mare named Honey. He hauled me up and sat me behind him on the saddle. One of the young cows made a break from the herd and started running down the dirt side road to Joe Kelly's place. Don glanced over his shoulder at me and said, "Hang on." At that point he kicked the horse and away we went, running at full speed after the stray cow, while my mother looked on in horror. I did hang on and discovered that I was not scared at all. In fact, it was the biggest thrill of my life. After that wild ride, Don decided that I could have my own horse. My mother bought me a small Morgan mare named Lucky at a horse auction in Powell. We rode together for many years, discovering most of the horse trails in the Shoshone National Forest.

In 1961, Don's family bought the Bradford Ranch, owned by Catherine Bradford McCelland and Frank McCelland. This place was located at the end of Green Creek overlooking the river, just around two miles from the main ranch where we were living. My mother, Don, and I then moved to the Bradford Ranch: a large lodge-type log house, a horse barn, corrals, many outbuildings, and a very large fenced-in chicken coop. My chores doubled, as did my mother's and Don's. We now had four milk cows, chickens, geese, horses, sheep, and cows to take care of. Don and I arose at 4:30 in the morning to milk the cows and feed the horses. The milk was separated (in a separating machine), and the milk was bottled by hand and distributed among the other family members. My mother made her own bread, and we churned our own butter. The number one rule on any ranch was that no one eats until the livestock has been taken care of and all the chores were completed. I have carried this rule with me throughout my life. In fact, most of the things I learned on the ranch have served me well in my adult life, the most important lesson being that of responsibility and reliability.

While living at the Bradford Ranch, I joined the 4-H Club. My first project was to bake a cake. I had obtained a recipe from Jake Royal, one of our close neighbors. With some instruction from my mother, I completed Jake's Philadelphia Red Cake. During the Park County Fair at the end of August, I entered a similar cake in the 4-H baking division at the County Fair and won a blue ribbon. Over the years at the ranch, I completed many 4-H projects. My most challenging project consisted of raising 50 bum lambs. These are lambs that have been rejected by their mothers in some fashion. My mother and I took over raising them, bottle feeding them three times a day and swamping out their pens. Lambs and calves are born during the worst possible conditions, usually in March and April, forcing us to supervise their births by staying up all night tending to them in the cold and windy weather that is so much a part of life in Wyoming. We had an assembly line organized with wooden troughs, which had holes in the bottom part where we inserted the bottles. We fed them in shifts, and with so many lambs, this took a great amount of time. During that spring, the weather was unusually horrible, and we had to move the lambs onto a closed-in porch attached to our house. I stayed home from school for a week during a spring blizzard to take care of the lambs. In the end, we raised all 50 lambs without losing one. Don and my mother took the lambs to the livestock auction in Powell that fall, and part of the money from their sale was put in a college fund for me.

OLIVE FELL

It is the weekend before the Fourth of July. Some say it will hit 90 today. I went to town early this morning to beat the heat. The drive home was tourists trying to pass on sections of the road where passing is not encouraged. Last week there was a bad accident by Trout Creek requiring the Jaws of Life and two ambulances. Rumor has it that poor judgment with passing was to blame.

The road from Cody to Yellowstone is packed with tourists, huge fifth-wheels, and giant tour buses three or four months out of the year. There is a steady stream of traffic seven days a week, all headed for Yellowstone and beyond. The most beautiful fifty miles in the United States, some say, and everyone is here to see it, though I don't see how they can when they speed through with only a destination in mind.

It wasn't always like this. When I first moved to Wyoming in 1959, there were tourists, of course, but not the onslaught we have today. There were no summer homes or subdivisions then, just ranches and hay fields. That time is long gone. I sit on my cabin porch listening to the summer traffic on the gravel county road, which has also increased. I close my eyes and imagine the valley the way it was in 1959, free from encroaching civilization. The Bradford Ranch is situated roughly a mile and a half from my cabin. The ranch house is now a Bed and Breakfast during tourist season. When I first moved back here in 2007, I thought about asking the owner if I could visit and walk around, but I haven't been able to work up the courage to do so. We were only there for six years, but it seemed like a lifetime to me. I miss the horses the most. I learned to ride at age ten. By age eleven I was riding with the cowboys, herding cattle and sheep, running down stray calves, going to horse auctions with my stepfather, and arranging wilderness pack trips with my mother. My horses were my life. My favorite horse, Missy, was a golden-brown Quarter Horse with a wide white stripe down her face. I took her to the Park County 4-H fair one year, and she won a big purple ribbon for Best In Show. Sadly, a few years later, she died of an intestinal impaction.

Life on the ranch was a long series of births and deaths, and all the things in between. There was branding, castrating, docking, pulling calves, dehorning, and butchering. All ranch kids had to face the fact that their favorite steer or lamb would be killed, butchered, and wrapped in white paper to be placed in the freezer. The barn always contained a deer or elk carcass hanging from the rafters. Don't even get me started with the chicken killings. My mother chopped their heads off with an ax and shoved them under a tin bucket until they stopped thrashing and bleeding. The harsh realities of life in Wyoming. One became immune to any feelings of love for these animals. Today, I can't stand to kill anything. I rescue spiders from the bathtub and carry them outside. My meat consumption is minimal at best. I even have trouble with mouse traps, although my husband takes care of that chore for me.

I learned to cook when I was participating in 4-H Club activities. My mother cooked all day Sunday, preparing meals and bread for the week ahead. Twice during the summer Don hired a crew of three or four men to help with the haying. My mother and I cooked breakfast, lunch and dinner for them during their four or five-day stay. It was exhausting to say the least, but we got it done. I was always baking something — cakes, cinnamon rolls, cookies, banana bread, brownies. We had a garden and a root cellar. We canned everything we could get our hands on. We picked chokecherries and gooseberries to make jam and jelly. Food production was an endless chore on the ranch.

Ranch life was never dull. During the summers, we trailed our cows across the river to graze on a BLM lease under Jim Mountain. This trek took all day, and we rode back late in the evening. I spotted a light at the top of a ridge on the northeast side of the valley and asked my stepfather if someone lived up there. He told me that was Olive Fell's house. He told me a few stories about Olive and used words like "cantankerous" and "feisty." Apparently, his family and Olive had gotten into a few arguments about trailing the cows through her property and Olive had won. There was mention of a shotgun being brought out at some point. He told me she was an artist and lived up there away from everybody by herself. He said she was a tough old bird and a very good artist.

She keeps to herself, he said, and she doesn't let anybody get away with anything.

Sometimes on the road to town, we would pass Olive in her old pickup truck. She was a short little woman who wore round glasses and an old straw hat. She could barely see over the steering wheel. There were always dogs riding with her, hanging out the window, panting and barking. From the porch on our ranch, we could see her light. I sat on the porch late in the evenings, staring up at it, wondering about all the stories and rumors.

I did not meet Olive Fell until the mid 1970s. After high school, I went away to college. My mother and stepfather gave up the ranch in 1967 and built a house just west of Green Creek. I sat on their porch many times and could see the light shining out from Olive's house. My mother became ill, and I moved back from college in 1974 to help take care of her. After she died, my friend Mark Spragg and I took a job as caretakers of a huge "summer house" owned by rich people from New York. This house was built on part of Olive Fell's property, way up under Jim Mountain. Olive, it seems, had struck a deal when she sold the property that she would be allowed to live there in her own house until she died. Mark said one day, "Why don't you call Olive and see if you can go over there and talk to her?" I was nervous about that, but I did call her. She was very friendly and said, Yes, of course, come over tomorrow.

The next day, I walked the half mile over to her house. It was a log house, with large picture windows on the west side. Olive came to the door, slightly disheveled and out of breath. I'm so glad you came! I need someone to clean, perhaps you would be interested? I said I would be glad to clean for her. She sat me down at her kitchen table and made toasted English muffins spread with plain yogurt and strawberry jam. We had tea. A small Pekinese with bad teeth crawled into my lap. Olive and I looked at each other across the table. I had expected someone more frightening. Not the slightly overweight woman with short reddish hair sitting across from me.

She looked like a little barn owl. She started out by saying that she had known my mother. You look just like her, she said. A very courageous woman, your mother, and very outspoken. I laughed out loud at that understatement. And now you're up here. How do you like it? I said I liked this view of the valley. I told her about looking up at her light all through my childhood, wondering who lived up here. And now you know, she chuckled.

She took me on a tour of the house. The living room was her studio, very sparsely furnished, with a white tile floor. An easel stood on the east end of the room with an unfinished painting of an elk propped up on it. There were two bathrooms with white and pale green tile. I don't remember the entire layout, but everything was absolutely spotless and I wondered why she needed anyone to clean. But we struck a deal anyway and I was to come and clean on Wednesday for $6.00 an hour, which she insisted on paying. I didn't want any money for the honor of cleaning Olive Fell's house, but I agreed. Walking home after our visit, I felt exhilarated and light on my feet.

Over the next few months, I went over to Olive's

every Wednesday to clean. I cleaned for about two hours, and then she summoned me for toasted English muffins and tea. We sat at the kitchen table and talked. Olive told me about her childhood. She and her brother Bill and their parents at one time lived in a dugout outside of Meeteetse. She talked about the brutal winters and the wind. How she almost died from a ruptured appendix because they were snowed in and couldn't go to the hospital in town. She spoke of her father, a brutal man who beat her and her brother. "He broke Bill," she said, "but he didn't break me." She talked about hardship and struggle.

Putting herself through art school in Chicago. Traveling to Europe. Meeting famous artists. She lectured me on the spiritualism of creativity. She showed me her etchings and paintings. I found her completely enthralling.

After two years, my life took another turn, and I moved down off the mountain to a house on Dunn Creek. I saw Olive just before I left. She fixed the usual muffins and tea and we sat and talked. As I was leaving she said, "You are a bright and shining light, but you hide it. Don't let anyone do that to you. You have the courage. Don't forget that, dear. " She patted my arm. I had tears in my eyes.

A few more years passed. I had a job working in the emergency room at West Park Hospital. One evening, the ambulance driver came downstairs to sit with me. "We just brought in Olive Fell," he said. "She had a stroke. She's not doing very well. " Panic overtook me. "I have to go see her," I said. He shook his head. "She wouldn't know you. She's in a coma." We got busy then with another ambulance call, and I worked late into the night. On the drive home, I looked for her light, but her house was dark. There was no beacon shining down for me. I cried all the way home.

Olive Fell died a few days later. I left the valley soon after that and moved to New Mexico. I spent thirty years in the southwest, started a successful business, bought a house, established myself, and struggled with the stress of living in a big crime-ridden city. I always remembered Olive's advice to me about courage. I longed for Wyoming and the day I would return to the valley after such a long exile.

That day finally came for me on July 10, 2007. Greg and I sold our houses, packed up a U-Haul, and moved back to the cabin on Green Creek. From the porch of the cabin I have a clear view of Olive Fell's house, perched up on the ridge overlooking the valley. I don't know who owns it now or if anyone lives there. Things have changed in this valley. More housing developments, people moving in from everywhere. None of them know the valley as it was when I came here so many years ago. No one remembers the ranching, the hard winters, the Saturday night potluck dinners at the schoolhouse, or the sparsity of neighbors.

In the late afternoon, I sit on the cabin porch and look up at her house. The last glowing rays of orange sunlight touch Olive's studio windows, the only light there now. I wish someone would leave Olive's studio light on, even though no one is there. That bright light would shine through the massive windows. I would sit on the porch looking out across the valley. Greg would ask me, "Who lives up there?" And I would smile and say, "That's Olive Fell's light."

CANDY

It is 5:30 in the morning. I am driving back from the airport in Cody, where I just deposited my 80-year-old sister. Every July for the last five years, Candy came from Tennessee to visit me at the cabin on Green Creek for one week. We would sit on the porch and look out at Jim Mountain and reminisce. Most of her sentences begin with "remember when?"

Remember when Mum scared the moose with her loud belching? Remember when I drank out of the horse tank on our trail ride? Remember when we were camping in Yellowstone and the bears climbed up on the roof of our car? Every year it's the same stuff. This year, however, would be her last visit here. She has a walker now and is very weak and wobbly. She arrived with a terrible cough and a fever of 100.7. She was extremely short of breath (more so than usual). I promptly took her to the Emergency Room, where we spent four hours while the ER staff ran every test known to mankind, including a COVID test. The diagnosis was acute bronchitis, worsening of her congestive heart failure, and extremely low potassium, which was the cause of her shortness of breath and weakness. She was given extra potassium pills and an inhaler treatment from Respiratory Therapy. When I finally got her into the car, she demanded that we get a chocolate milkshake at Dairy Queen. On the drive home, she said, "What do you suppose is wrong with me?"

Every year when she visits, she would ask me to help her move back to Wyoming. I remind her that she is living with her 91-year-old husband who has Parkinson's and is being well-cared for by her stepdaughter, Betsy. Betsy bought a house for them. Betsy takes them both to their various doctors' appointments. Betsy runs errands for them and brings them food. Betsy manages all the home care and the nurse visits, all while maintaining a full-time job as a teacher and tutoring kids in the evening. I tell Candy that she is much better off there than here. She begins to cry and says, "You're probably right."

For much of our lives, Candy and I were not close, either geographically or spiritually. We were nine years apart in age. On our trek to Wyoming, Candy was eighteen years old, and I was nine. We fought all the time. I teased her unmercifully and picked on her. She was gullible and an easy mark. There was a lot of yelling from our mother as she tried to break up the taunting fights. For me, Wyoming was an exciting adventure. For Candy, it was an intolerable situation. She got a job at JCPenney, but was fired after a few months because she had no math skills and was unable to make change or run the cash register. I never understood why our mother made Candy come with us. She wanted to stay with our grandmother and continue her relationship with her boyfriend. Instead, she did come to Wyoming with us and met Bob Livermore, the brother of John Livermore, the man who was head of the school board.

Bob and John lived with their mother, Ruth. Candy married Bob, and later in life told me that he was the worst mistake she had ever made. Both Virginia and Ruth opposed the marriage. Ruth told my mother that Bob was "not to be trusted around women," which became evident shortly after the wedding. He had no boundaries and pursued other women right in front of Candy. But they proceeded with the wedding, and Candy and Bob went back to New Hampshire to live on the South Hampton farm. Shortly after Candy's wedding, our mother married Don.

Candy and I never had much of a chance. We were thrown into relationships with abusive people who tried their best to make our lives hard. I feel like I have come out ahead, but Candy faced more difficulty. My mother's criticism and disapproval affected Candy more deeply than they did me. I remember one Thanksgiving we visited the New England farmhouse where Candy and Bob were living. Candy had gotten a turkey, but that was about it. When my mother found out there was nothing else to go with our dinner, she scolded Candy repeatedly. Mother and I drove to the grocery store in Amesbury and bought potatoes and green beans. Candy cried all day, off and on, hurt deeply by my mother's harsh words. Years later, when I visited her at the Missouri farm where she lived with her second husband, Keith, she made a venison roast in the crockpot. I gently suggested that we start some baked potatoes and make a salad. She seemed surprised she hadn't thought of that. Our mother's constant verbal abuse left Candy feeling uncertain and confused — not just about cooking, but about everything. She struggled to think ahead, would get flustered and cry. She could not deal with the past and carried tremendous regrets. She was as hard on herself as mother was.

Growing up with Don and Virginia, I was always on edge, constantly worried that I had unknowingly angered them. Their accusations often blindsided me — I thought I was doing fine, only for them to suddenly point out some terrible mistake I supposedly made. I was regularly blamed, chastised, or yelled at. I never felt good enough for my mother. She wanted me to achieve great things, to become someone I wasn't, and was always critical and disapproving. When she teamed up with Don, things only got worse.

When my grandmother died, my stepfather called me out into the driveway at the ranch. He had two letters in his hand, unopened, from my grandmother to me. I was twelve or thirteen at the time. I had put the letters aside, having much more interesting things to do on the ranch. Ride my horse, milk the cows, feed the sheep, gather the eggs. He held the letters out to me, telling me that Granny had died. "And you just threw her letters aside without any thought about how that would make her feel," he said. In other words, I was responsible for my grandmother's death because I had not immediately opened her letters. I'm sure my mother told him to do that. She was an expert at handing out guilt.

This was another painful example of being blamed

for something that was not my fault. I don't know what happened to those letters. I know I took them, hanging my head in shame, and ran off to read them by the creek. They were funny letters, stories about her cats or the flowers she and my Aunt Shirley had planted. At that age, I was beginning to find her letters a little silly. When I was nine, they were interesting, but I was beginning to outgrow them. I always read them and answered them eventually. Just not that time.

There is enough guilt to find on our own without anyone else handing it to us. I took that guilt, however, put it on my shoulders and carried it with me all these years. I still cry when I think of that day, of the letters and my stepfather telling me how to feel.

I felt that if anyone should have felt guilty, it should have been my mother. She took me away from Granny, moved me to Wyoming, and didn't plan on taking me back. She wanted to get me away from my grandmother's influence. What did she expect would happen? Of course I would start to grow apart from the New England family. I see now that she was lashing out at me because she was feeling the burden of her own guilt.

When we came to Wyoming in 1959, our lives were forever changed. Our destinies were decided. Candy started down an exhausting path with the Livermores. Virginia took up with Don. I grew up here in this valley, confused and struggling. After I graduated from high school in 1968, I went away to college, came back, went away again, and now I'm back home to stay. Every day brings a new realization and personal revelations about my childhood. Events that began here in this valley carried over into other places, other lives. It has been a long haul for me. My decisions may not have always been right. But right or wrong, who can tell? You choose a path and take a direction, wondering all along if you're doing the right thing. Have I been a good person? Am I following the rules correctly? Should I be proud of myself, or should I wallow in self-despair at all my mistakes and blunders? I have gone over and over all these questions in therapy so many times, I am sick of thinking about them. Something tells me to go forward without looking back. The people who abused us are dead. I can breathe a sigh of relief and try to live out my life in peace. The answer is that I should just let it all go and move ahead with my life, one day at a time.

Candy died at the age of 81 on March 15, 2023. I flew down to Tennessee to see her on February 6th, essentially to say good-bye. Betsy told me that she was winding down. Candy was in a nursing home, bedridden, not eating, wasting away. When I walked into the room, she recognized me and seemed to perk up a little bit. I sat with her and we reminisced about the New Hampshire farm. Dementia had taken quite a bit of her memory. I brought her chocolate milkshakes. I refilled the bird feeder outside her window. Two days later when I flew back to Wyoming, I couldn't stop myself from sobbing as I held her hand and said good-bye. She patted my hand and said, "I know." As I left the room she said, "See you later, alligator." I cried for a long time in the car.

AUNTIE

It is April 1998. I am visiting my Aunt Shirley who is confused and spinning in her Alzheimer's state, thinking that she is in a hotel instead of a nursing home, asking when she can go home. We don't answer her, but instead change the subject to something she is more able to deal with, such as the past. She can recall things from her childhood quite clearly. She asks how Virginia is doing, not realizing that Virginia died in 1975. I am deeply saddened by the decline of Auntie's sanity, another loss piled on top of all the things gone from me that I cherished the most.

Auntie developed Alzheimer's at age 78, although it may have been earlier than that as she was an expert at covering up. Shirley lived in West Newton in a two-story house with a huge backyard. Originally, my grandmother lived there with my mother, my sister and me. When Virginia moved Candy and me to Wyoming in 1959, Auntie moved from her Park Avenue apartment in Boston to West Newton to be with Granny. After Granny died, Shirley lived there by herself. Shirley was married briefly to Albert Charait at the beginning of WWII. He was a Lieutenant in a paratrooper unit, but was killed in action in Holland. Shirley never remarried, living alone for the rest of her life.

Aunt Shirley worked as an occupational therapist for many years. She specialized in working with stroke victims. She developed splints for use in her patients' rehabilitation programs. She traveled extensively and enjoyed gardening and bird watching. Auntie, as we called her, sported a bumper sticker that said "I BRAKE FOR BOBOLINKS," and brake she did at any given time without warning, hurling us into the front seat like crash test dummies, nearly killing us all for the opportunity to identify a bird. She could spot a Blackburnian warbler at 100 yards. She knew every bird and every bird song. We spent many peaceful hours in the New Hampshire woods, listening and observing.

I saw my first Red Sox game at Fenway Park with Auntie. I was six years old at the time. Shirley was more than just an avid fan. She supplied me with a hot dog, a baseball cap, a pennant, and a bag of peanuts. She sat me down next to her and said, "Now we are going to watch the game." To me, this meant don't talk, don't ask to go to the bathroom, and don't run around. I don't remember what happened at that game, but I still watch the Red Sox to this day. As an adult, I called Auntie on Sunday afternoons to check in. "What are you doing?" I would ask. "Watching the damn Red Sox loose again," she would reply with disgust. Auntie and I had long conversations about the meaning of life and spiritualism. We talked about the latest art film, the newest issue of *The New Yorker*, the class she was taking on mind/body awareness.

Whenever I phoned her, she would answer saying "I *knew* you were going to call. I have so much to tell you."

Auntie was plagued by obsessive compulsive disorder, complete with checking the door locks and unplugging appliances numerous times every time she left the house. She had inherited the Evans-Swain worrying mechanism which she called "awfulizing." In any given situation, Auntie could come up with the most terrible scenario that could or might happen. She was stubborn and independent. With the onset of dementia, those qualities just got worse. We all saw the signs, but we couldn't do anything about it. Auntie refused any suggestion, saying "Yes, but ...," coming up with every excuse she could think of why she shouldn't or couldn't do something we wanted her to do. Our cousin, Caroline Evans, who lived nearby in West Newton, was able to convince her not to drive, only after Shirley had side-swiped all the parked cars along her street. Shirley sold her car to next-door neighbor for one dollar. Then she called the police because she forgot she had sold him the car, thinking that he had stolen it. In fact, the police were called frequently by neighbors because Auntie was locked out of her house or was seen walking down the street to the corner store barefoot, wearing only her nightgown.

We first noticed that something was wrong with Auntie when she stopped sending us our Christmas and birthday checks. She always sent a card and $25.00 without fail. When we called her on the phone (an old-fashioned dial phone because she refused to use a push-button one), she picked up the receiver and held it upside down, and thus being unable to hear anything, she would hang up. We would have to call back several times before she would pick it up correctly. Sometimes she would say, "Hang on. I have to brush my teeth," leaving us holding on, ultimately forgetting us, and we would have to hang up and try again, though her phone would then be off the hook for days. One time she told me she was trying to make a call to her friend in Arkansas, and the operator kept getting progressively testy with her. She was actually hearing the recorded message that said, "If you would like to make a call, please hang up and dial again." Auntie was trying to interact with the recording. Privately, my sister and I laughed about these incidents, but we were sad as well because we knew we were going to have to make decisions for Auntie which she would not like.

Loss of mind function is somehow worse than death, and the grief is longer-lasting. One cannot just grieve and go on because the shell of the person is still living. I expect them to suddenly snap out of it and start talking normally, but I know this is an impossible fantasy. People are living longer in today's world, but the quality of that longer life is in question. Auntie lost all awareness, and everything became a safety issue. We hired home care companions to be with her and help her with meals and cleaning, but she fired them immediately. She began falling, injuring herself quite badly several times. The State of Massachusetts stepped in and declared her an Elder At Risk. We had no choice but to place her in a nursing home. When she heard of our plans, she rallied to the point of calling me on the phone and blaming me for trying to "put her away." "You, of all people," she said. "I thought you would stand up for me." I told her I was standing up for her, that it was not safe for her to live alone. I told her she would have the best care we could find for her. She hung up on me.

On Auntie's 81st birthday, I traveled from Albuquerque to Missouri to visit her. She was in a nursing home in Kirksville where my sister worked as a Registered Nurse. My sister felt she could keep a better eye on things if our Auntie was there with her. There were other Alzheimer's patients in the nursing home, and the quality of the staff was high. Still, Shirley wanders the halls and picks up other people's belongings. She wears someone else's glasses. My sister tries to keep up with her, giving back the belongings and patiently retrieving the right pair of glasses.

There is a bird feeder outside Shirley's window where she watches finches, nuthatches, and chickadees, pointing them out to anyone who happens to be in the room.

I haven't seen Auntie for several months. She doesn't talk much at all now and she gets very distracted. Her eyes light up when I come into the room. I have brought flowers and chocolate. She says excitedly, "Ghirardelli!" when she sees the chocolate. My sister and I double over with laughter, realizing that in our family the recognition of chocolate will be the last thing to go.

Auntie laughs right along with us. "We love you, Auntie," my sister says. She stares at us and says emphatically, "Yes!"

In our family, no one ever said I love you. There was

no physical contact, no hugging, no expression of love for anyone, with the exception of my grandmother who hugged Candy and me often. My new family in Wyoming was just the same. No expression of love, just a lot of harsh criticism and constant disapproval. Shortly before we left for Wyoming, I went upstairs in the West Newton house where my grandmother was sitting in the dark in her rocking chair. I climbed onto her lap and hugged her. Her apron was damp from crying. "Why are you crying, Granny?" I asked. "Because you are leaving," she said. Years later, while I was living in Albuquerque, I got a phone call from Auntie. "I'm calling everyone who is left in the family and telling them that I love them," she said. From that day forward whenever we spoke, we ended the phone call saying "I love you." She had also called Candy with her message of love. Which prompted Candy and I to always say we loved each other whenever we spoke.

Auntie died in 2001. My grief was unbearable. I thought about her constantly. I remembered all the good things we had done together. When I visited her in West Newton, we would go to a foreign film cinema and watch the latest film with subtitles. I remember one in particular: a film called *Everybody's Fine*. The gist of the movie was about a widower who would try to keep in touch with his children by calling them by phone periodically. When he would ask how they were, they would reply saying "Everybody's fine," when in fact they were not fine. They didn't want to worry him. One day he decided to go and visit his children in person. He showed up unannounced and found to his dismay that they weren't fine by any means. We enjoyed the movie so much that whenever we spoke on the phone after that, we would say "everybody's fine" and laugh; our private joke for many years.

A couple of months after Auntie died, I was taking a nap and was in that in-between state of waking and sleeping. I heard her voice saying "Hello, dear." In my head, I said "Auntie is that you?" She replied "Yes, dear, I'm here." "Are you okay?" I asked. "Yes, dear, everybody's fine." I knew right away that it was Auntie talking to me in my head. She told me that the story I had just finished writing was very good and that I should keep writing. I asked about Virginia, but she said Virginia wasn't there. She said she had to go, but I was to remember that she loved me. "Good-bye dear," she said. "Good-bye Auntie," I said. After that experience, my grief went away. I felt only happiness that she had contacted me and that she was fine.

Several months later we buried Auntie's ashes in the Evans section of the cemetery in Amesbury, Massachusetts. Our cousin Caroline arranged the whole thing with a lovely luncheon at the Old Mill Restaurant in Amesbury. As we were all pulling into the parking lot of the cemetery, a huge Red Tail Hawk lifted out of one of the towering pine trees surrounding the cemetery. Caroline, Candy and I said in unison, "There goes Auntie!" We all agreed that day was one of the best in our lives.

GRANNY

It is October 26th, my mother's birthday. Jim Mountain is covered with fresh snow and fog. Winter is here. Tomorrow we may get six inches of snow at the cabin. I celebrate her birthday every year by being outside, taking a walk, hiking with the dogs or sitting by the creek listening to the chickadees calling to each other. Today I am sitting on the porch of my cabin, drinking coffee, taking in the fresh snow and the inevitable cold weather.

My grandmother would have hated Wyoming. The vast emptiness and soaring mountains would have terrified her. She was a New Englander through and through. The things I remember about my grandmother are these: she loved chocolate and used chocolate as a reward for Candy and me. If we finished our dinner, we got a chocolate. If we did our homework, we got a chocolate. She wore a house dress every day. I never saw her in pants of any kind. She wore heavy stockings and sturdy black walking shoes. She always had a full over-the-head apron covering her dress. She wore her curly black-and-graying hair rolled up with hairpins, making a kind of halo around her head. She loved to cook huge meals. Her Sunday dinners consisted of a roast chicken, mashed potatoes, fresh peas and homemade bread. Most of all, she loved her flower garden where she spent hours weeding and transplanting.

Granny was a talented writer. She kept a journal while she was living in South Hampton on the farm. She titled her journals *Letters to My Great Grandchildren*. Aunt Shirley typed them up for us and had them bound in a book after Granny died. She also wrote children's stories, that I have in an old-fashioned black notebook and which I keep meaning to type into my computer, but haven't done so as yet. Granny made hooked rugs with Grandma Moses-like country farm scenes depicting our South Hampton farm including all of us sledding or riding in the horse-drawn sleigh with dogs running after us and playing. Her biggest accomplishment was her transformation of the Fitz house, built in the late 1700s, into a home for elderly people. She called it "Fitz Memorial." She took in "borders" in her own house and used the money to fix up her nursing home, which was a great success in the community.

Despite the fact that Granny was a hard-working, talented woman, she worried constantly about things that could happen to us, her cats, her dogs and her family. I remember her telling me not to eat apple skins because that was known to cause appendicitis. Hence, if I wanted an apple, she would peel it for me. Whenever any of us left the house to go to school or work, she worried all day until we got home safely. When Virginia decided to teach school in Wyoming, Granny was overwhelmed with worry about what would happen to us. In retrospect, the Wyoming adventure made us stronger. Yes, some bad things did happen to us, but we persevered. I would not change the past. The past is what made me who I am today — a strong, capable woman who is not afraid of anything. When I catch myself worrying, I think of Granny and I close my eyes and say "this, too, shall pass." Despite her overwhelming sense of disaster, I miss Granny. I think about her fondly. I wish I could have seen her before she died. My last memory of her standing on the sidewalk waving as we pulled away on our journey into the future haunts me.

DON

June 2008. It is the second day of summer at my Green Creek cabin. Sitting on the porch with my coffee and my smoke, I feel my body relax. I take a deep breath and let the peace and quiet of the morning slide over me. We have had rain the past few days, making the lawn vividly green. Robins hunt for worms around the sprinkler heads. Horse trailers pulled by duel-wheeled pickups chug up the county road. The early-morning sun filters through the tall sagebrush which surrounds the cabin, protecting me from the outside world. This will be a good day.

The summer mornings here make nine months of winter more bearable. Here in the valley there is no world economic crisis. The peace of being here erases all the nasty, angry people in the outside world. There is nothing here but the earth and nature, in balance, quietly going ahead with life. Nothing changes. The mountains are still here every morning when I wake up. The creek still runs. Bald eagles still circle high above the west mesa. The cabin on Green Creek has always been my touchstone. I can count on it being here, comforting me, putting its arms around me and telling me everything is going to be all right. During the time I lived in New Mexico, I dreamed of returning to the cabin in this valley. Now that dream has become a reality.

I remember everything about my childhood. But sometimes I find that I recall events wrong. Sometimes I remember only the bad things. It is hard to say whether the happy times outnumbered the bad times. I have learned, after years of therapy, to look at all events equally without judgment, as if I were viewing a documentary about someone else's life. I have learned to look for the truth without fear or sadness. Most importantly, I have learned not to assign blame.

When my mother married Don, she wrote a long letter of explanation to Granny and Shirley. Aunt Shirley took the news quite badly, as she realized she was going to be the only caregiver for my grandmother. My grandmother, after reading the letter, had to be hospitalized with chest pain. Shirley wrote my mother a scathing letter, vowing never to forgive her. She and Virginia did not speak for a number of years. My grandmother recovered and we spoke on the phone quite often, and although Shirley did talk with me, she would not speak to her sister.

Don and Virginia and I lived on the ranch for six years. Don was a respected member of the ranching community. Don taught me how to fish. He played marbles with me after dinner. We played board games and penny-ante poker. We did chores together and he taught me how to drive the hay truck while he threw hay to the livestock. The three of us explored Yellowstone in the summertime. We went on pack trips and Don took me hunting in the fall. I learned how to gut a deer and how to cut up the meat and package it.

In the fall of 1964, Virginia took a job teaching in Gillette, which was a 4½ hour drive from Cody. Don hauled their camper trailer to Gillette and she stayed there during the week, driving home on some weekends, but not every weekend, as winter driving over the Big Horns was not something she wanted to do. So Don and I were on our own. I did most of the cooking. I remember driving into town with him to get groceries one weekend. I had meant to buy bacon, but instead chose a package that turned out to be salt pork. That evening I cooked it as bacon and made scrambled eggs and toast. Later that night, I woke up feeling very sick to my stomach and ended up vomiting, probably from the fatty salt pork. Don got up to see if I was okay. I threw up repeatedly, finally staggering into my room to lie down. I drifted off a few times and then suddenly I felt Don get under the covers with me. Then just as suddenly, I felt his hand under my nightgown and his finger in my vagina. "This is how your mother likes it," he said. "You know, the walls are thin and we can hear you masturbating sometimes." At that point I flew out of the bed and ran into the bathroom and locked the door. I don't know how long I stayed in the bathroom. Don stood outside the door and told me that he would never "go all the way with me." I didn't know what that meant, but I was terrified. I sat on the cold tile floor, hugging my knees to my chest, crying. Then he told me this was our little secret and I was not to tell my mother. After some time had passed, I cautiously opened the door and ran into my room. He had gone back to his room.

My whole life shifted with the fondling episode. The stepfather, whom I admired and, yes, loved, was a child molester. I didn't know the meaning of "molester" and I didn't know what was happening. I had no words for this type of situation. This was surreal to me. I couldn't handle it with any normal emotion. I had no idea that people could behave this way. I trusted all adults involved in my life completely. I remember feelings of abandonment, vulnerability, and humiliation. Nothing could ever be the same. I lost all respect for him. I had been left with a man I trusted and who had let me down completely. I was not safe and protected. I was alone and endangered. My mother was oblivious to the situation, thinking the same thing — that I was safe with Don, that he was trustworthy.

I remember standing at the window in my bedroom, looking out on the bleak winter landscape, wondering how to escape, how to stay safe. It never occurred to me to run away. I could not have left my mother. I retreated into depression and moodiness. When my mother returned from Gillette, she saw the change in me. She kept after me about what happened to the friendship I had with Don. Why was I so angry all the time? What happened to the games of marbles and checkers? She blamed it all on puberty, but I knew better. I never spoke directly to Don again. I couldn't look him in the eye. I spent all my time trying to avoid being alone with him. I couldn't tell my mother about him. I was certain that she would blame me somehow. Ironically, soon after my mother married, my step cousin, Judi, took me aside and told me never, never to be alone with Cecil. She said he had tried to rape her when she was fourteen. She had managed to escape to a neighbor's house, and when she told her father what had happened, he seemed to just shrug it off. I remember driving up the driveway with my mother. In the backyard we saw Cecil and Dorothy standing close together. Dorothy had her arms around Cecil's neck and their foreheads were touching. My mother looked over at me and said, "Now that is not right." I had been warned about Cecil, but no one warned me about Don. Perhaps no one knew.

My excellent memory has failed me as to what happened after "the incident." I do remember Don driving me over to Gillette one Saturday to see my mother. She was living in her little travel trailer behind the school where she taught. She had her Dachshund, Hansi, with her. When we got to the trailer, she told me to take Hansi and go for a long walk. I was gone so long they came looking for me. I was sitting by an old falling-down barn with Hansi, probably about a half mile from her trailer. I was crying. My mother asked me what was wrong. I could see Don stiffen. I didn't answer, but I got up and headed back to her trailer with them following along behind me.

For the rest of the school year, Don and I kept our distance from each other. I still fixed dinner for us and I did all my chores along with him in the mornings. I walked up the lane to wait for the school bus half an hour earlier than necessary. I made excuses to stay in town after school and catch a ride home with a neighbor who commuted to Cody every day for work. I spent a lot of time in my room doing homework.

A few weeks after my mother returned from Gillette, she discovered a dimpling in her right breast. Biopsy showed breast cancer and she had a mastectomy, radiation and chemotherapy in Billings. Aunt Shirley flew out immediately to be with her and help out. Apparently, they were talking again. The incident with Don was put on the back burner. I started to block it out because I wanted to focus on helping my mother. Having my Aunt Shirley there was a big deal.

I had not seen her for almost four years. We were all trying to be positive and upbeat for my mother. As it turned out, after months of treatment, my mother was pronounced cancer-free. My aunt returned to West Newton and they wrote letters back and forth. I started high school in the fall. My mother felt well enough to return to teaching at Northwest Community College in Powell. Cancer had given her a new lease on life. She began writing again and wrote an article for the *Denver Post Sunday Section*, entitled "Cancer Gave Me Wings."

HIGH SCHOOL AND BEYOND

It is the beginning of another winter at the cabin, November 2023. Greg and I have been living here for sixteen years. It doesn't seem possible that it has been that long since we packed up and moved to Green Creek, leaving our New Mexico lives behind us forever. It is hard, too, to accept the fact that I am 73 years old. It has been a long journey from 1959 to today. I feel as though I have lived many lifetimes throughout this time period. And yet, at times, I am still the frightened fourteen-year-old girl clutching her knees to her chest, crying on the bathroom floor.

High school was sort of a blur for me. I was socially awkward and painfully shy. I did join the high school choir and blossomed under the direction of our choir teacher, Paul Hanselmann. But I had no friends, except for Karen and Connie Krone. Ranch kids were usually ostracized because they had to ride the bus and couldn't stay after school for any social activities. I was a good student and made the Honor Roll almost every month. During the summer months I worked at some of the dude ranches on the North Fork. Connie and I first started working at the Trail Shop Inn. We cleaned cabins and served dinners in the dining room to our guests. My depression lifted somewhat because I was away from the ranch and my parents. I actually felt happy and enjoyed my summer jobs. We attended musicals and square dances at Rimrock Ranch, which was a short walk from the Trail Shop. Life was beginning to be fun again.

When I was a Junior in high school, I started to notice boys. In particular, I noticed Doug Headlee, a senior, who drove a black '56 Chevy. His mother, Edith, was a teacher at Eastside School and was a friend of my mother's, which probably was the reason why I was allowed to date him. He was also willing to drive 25 miles to the ranch on a Saturday night to pick me up for a date, and then 25 miles back to Cody after dropping me off at the 11:00 p.m. curfew. Doug and I dated throughout the school year. I went to his senior prom with him. I lost my virginity in the back seat of the '56 Chevy that night. At the end of the school year, Doug gave me a "friendship ring," of which Virginia and Edith did not approve. Doug then moved to Denver to attend airline school. I worked at Grizzly Ranch cleaning cabins that summer. Doug and I wrote a few letters back and forth, but then we drifted apart. During the late summer of 1967, Virginia and Don finally had enough of Cecil and the ranch. Cecil had hired another ranch manager without telling Don. Cecil had sold off a lot of the ranch land in order to pay his debts. We moved out of the main lodge and into the small caretaker's cabin across the road from the ranch. Don and Virginia were compensated for their years of ranch work with 40 acres of sagebrush covered hills just south of the main ranch where Mary and Jim still lived. Don bought a backhoe and began construction on a house on this 40 acres. He also began a business with the backhoe and did quite well in the valley for many years. At the end of the summer they had a full covered basement constructed. We moved all our belongings into that basement.

Virginia had taken another teaching job in Powell River, British Columbia. We boarded our four remaining horses with a neighbor and left the ranch for good.

My mother insisted that I travel to British Columbia with them, where she would begin her new teaching job and I would begin my senior year at the Powell River High School. I was not happy about this decision and I went along with it reluctantly. I did not want to leave Cody High School, where I had favorite teachers and a few friends. But the trip to Powell River was a new adventure to which I begrudgingly agreed. We drove my mother's new Plymouth Fury to Vancouver, BC where we took a ferry to Powell River. The ferry was the only way to get there, and Powell River was at the very end of the ferry stop. We arrived during a heavy rain which continued, off and on, throughout early fall and into winter. The sun rarely broke through the heavy clouds and mist. Everything was damp and dripping. We rented a small house on the outskirts of town in the middle of a rain forest, complete with huge ferns and gigantic soggy cedar trees. The house was old and damp. The roof leaked and there was mold everywhere.

The high school there was old and damp as well. There was no choir for me to join and I did not fit in. My depression deepened and I repeatedly asked my mother to let me go back to Cody. I was desperately homesick for Wyoming. She finally relented, and at the Christmas break I flew back to Cody. My friend, Connie Krone, was two years older than me, and had already graduated from high school. After multiple conversations with Connie and her mother, I was allowed to stay with Connie while I finished high school.

She worked as a dental hygienist for a local orthodontist. She had a small one-bedroom apartment near the hospital. She also had a car. She picked me up at the Cody airport and drove me to her apartment. We got caught up on all the gossip. I re-enrolled in my high school Senior Class after the holiday break. My mother sent Connie a check every month for my half of the rent. I was very glad to be away from Don and Virginia. Things were so tense between Don and me, I had no alternative but to leave.

Leaving British Columbia and traveling back to Cody on my own was a major turning point in my life. I was free of Don and Virginia. I knew that I would never have to live with them again. I was sad to have lost the ranch, but I was back with my friends and my classmates. I wanted my last year of high school to be my best. I got straight A's in all my classes. I participated in musicals and concerts with the choir and joined a madrigal quartet.

Connie and I were too young to go to bars, so the only entertainment we had was driving up and down Cody's main street, honking at people we knew. This activity was officially called "bugging main." We usually ended up at Bud's Drive-In which was where most high school kids congregated. On one particular Saturday night in March, we were driving up and down main street looking for boys, when we spotted a spiffy-looking '68 Camaro parked at Bud's Drive-In. Connie pulled up beside it and rolled her window down. After a brief conversation, she parked her car out of the way at the back of the drive-in lot. We got in the backseat of the Camaro and started talking to the two young men who were in the car. Duane, the driver, and Jerry, his passenger, were from Powell. We drove around town for a while, talking and drinking beer. We ended up in the Cody Café where the boys bought us cheeseburgers and fries. They asked for our phone number, took us back to our car, and drove away, assuring us that they would give us a call.

Driving back to the apartment, Connie and I reviewed the information we had received from the two young men. They were good-looking young men. Jerry was tall, blond, blue-eyed, and he had that Robert Redford look. Duane was also tall, tanned, and wore glasses (as did Connie). Duane and Jerry had gone to high school together. After high school they enlisted in the army. Duane went to Viet Nam and Jerry went to work on an army base. Duane worked in an office in Viet Nam and never saw any action. After their year was up, they returned to Powell, lived with their parents and got jobs. Duane bought the Camaro and Jerry bought a midnight blue 1968 Mercury Cougar. They called us the next day to make a date for the following Saturday. Duane had paired up with Connie and Jerry paired up with me. Connie told them how to get to our apartment.

They planned to pick us up at 5:00, take us to dinner, and then to a movie at the downtown Cody theater. We were so excited to actually have a real date. We went to JCPenny and bought some new clothes. I could barely keep it together during the week, going to classes and daydreaming about Saturday night.

JERRY

Yesterday was my 74th birthday. I am struggling with this damned memoir. I have found myself lost in memories, trying to sort out which ones are important and which are just distractions. I have been told that I have an eidetic memory, remembering feelings and surroundings more than just a photographic memory. Sometimes this ability to remember everything gets in the way.

When Connie and I met Duane and Jerry our fates were sealed. Connie married Duane a year and a half later, and they moved to California. After graduation from high school, I spent the summer working for Don and Barbara Keller at River's Rest Ranch. In September, I went to Arizona State University for my first year of college where I discovered marijuana and alcohol and spent that first year partying with all the other students who were celebrating being away from their parents. I managed to get a B average in all my classes, although from what I learned at the party school, that was pretty normal for everyone. Technically, Jerry and I were still dating, although we only spoke on the phone occasionally. He drove to Tempe over the Christmas break and we spent some time together getting to know Phoenix and the surrounding area. He left looking very depressed and concerned that I was drifting away from him. However, when I came home in May, we picked up where we left off. I was still staying at Connie's apartment, although she was working or off with Duane most of the time.

Jerry and I spent a lot of time together, and he also met Don and Virginia. My mother was very impressed with Jerry and encouraged our relationship. When Don and Virginia came back from British Columbia, they completed their house and Jerry and I helped them with some of the landscaping. Jerry built a sloping rock wall for them with lichen-covered rock that Don and Virginia had collected over the years. I was considering getting a job at one of the dude ranches in the valley. But around the end of July, I discovered that I was pregnant. I saw a doctor in Billings because I was throwing up all the time and I felt awful. He informed me that I was around five weeks along in a pregnancy. This was quite a shock for Jerry and for me. This was not the age of open sexual discussion. Birth control was never mentioned. Pregnancy out of wedlock was still considered shameful and indecent. I was desperate. Jerry and I made a plan to go to Oregon and give the baby up for adoption. Why we came to this decision was unclear to me. Jerry never suggested that we get married. I only remember the fact that I wanted to keep this a secret from my parents and, in order to do that, we would have to leave for Oregon. We lied to everyone and said we were going to get married along the way. Here was another life-changing decision staring me in the face. Every time I thought of doing the right thing, telling my parents and keeping the baby, I came back around to Oregon. As it turned out, it was the right thing to do, but I didn't realize that until many years later.

Jerry and I packed up his car and left for Oregon around the middle of August. I was having a hard time concealing the enlarging belly and my mother commented that I looked like I was gaining weight. I shrugged it off, saying probably too much beer and burgers. Despite our escape to Oregon being a desperate act, it was also a Big Adventure. We had heard good things about Oregon. My Aunt Shirley sent me $2500 as a wedding present. Virginia gave us $1000. When we got to Eugene, Oregon, we found a small efficiency apartment for $350 a month. We explored Eugene and Portland. Jerry got a good job at a sawmill making about $1200 a month which was excellent pay for that area. I got fatter and bought two maternity tops and a pair of stretchy pants. I made some money by babysitting for some of the tenants in the apartment complex.

The doctor I saw in Billings had given me the name of Jack Bell, MD as a good choice for an OB-GYN. I made an appointment with him and told him that I was giving the baby up for adoption. He gave me the name of an attorney who handled adoptions. By the end of October all plans were in order and adoptive parents had been found. In those days adoption was completely secret. I had no say in who the adoptive family would be. The adoption papers were sealed by the court. I could only hope that my baby would be well cared for and happy.

My state of mind during the pregnancy is somewhat blurry. I stayed home most of the time, only venturing out on weekends when Jerry would drive us around exploring new places. We did not want anyone to know who we were or what we were doing. I don't remember talking to Jerry about what I was feeling or what he was feeling. We were killing time, waiting for the birth to be over so we could get on with our lives. I was planning on taking some classes at the University of Oregon. Jerry wanted to use the GI Bill to take classes there as well. I wrote letters to my mother and my aunt, lying about how we were doing. I told them that I had a job at JCPenny and I was taking classes at U of O.

Somehow we got through the holidays and winter. As an added bonus, it rained almost constantly, and the dreariness of my situation was only amplified by the weather. Early in the morning of March 15, 1970 I began to have contractions and Jerry drove me to the hospital. He did not go inside with me, but dropped me off at the curb and drove away. I checked in and was taken to Labor and Delivery. After being shaved and prepped, my labor suddenly stopped. Dr. Bell wanted to send me home, but I told him I was alone and I would have to take a taxi home. They decided to keep me, and I walked the hallways hoping to get things going again. After six hours, they started me on a Pitocin drip. At 5:05 p.m., I had my 5-pound baby girl all alone at Sacred Heart Hospital in Eugene Oregon. As was the case in most adoptions, I was not allowed to hold my baby. I was able to look at her for a few seconds as the nurse held her up. She had a mop of curly black hair, like me. She was crying and I held out my hand to her as she was whisked out of the room. I cried, too, as the doctor sutured my episiotomy.

I stayed in the hospital for three days. I very seldom slept. One night at about 11:00 p.m. I was standing at the window and I saw Jerry driving slowly by the hospital. At least he was thinking about me. On the third day, a lawyer came to my room with the final papers to sign. I couldn't read them through my tears so I just made a stab at signing them. I took a taxi back to the apartment. It was dark and unkempt, dirty dishes in the sink, drapes closed. When Jerry came home from work, I was lying down in the bedroom. He came in and lay down beside me. He was crying. He said, "I want my baby girl." I remember anger boiling up inside me when he said that. Why didn't he tell me that before we put her up for adoption? I remained angry with him for some time afterwards. I sat in the apartment for days without looking outside.

Somehow, we began to pull ourselves out of our depression. I went back to school and found a job in a dress shop at one of the malls. Jerry went to school as well, studying architecture. I changed my major from psychology to English literature. Jerry and I were getting along quite well. We never talked about the baby, although my anger quietly festered for months. About a year later, I told Jerry I wanted to get my own apartment. He seemed to agree with this arrangement. He co-signed a car loan for me for a 1969 Camaro. I found a studio apartment fairly close to the University. We still saw each other, actually going back to dating, but I was on my own and that was a good feeling. However, he told my mother when she called one day that I had moved out. She immediately flew out from Wyoming to "mediate" the situation. We did not want or need her interference, but there she was trying to get us back together. We tried to explain that we were still together, just living separately, which she didn't believe. She stayed with Jerry at his apartment and, while she was there, I was terrified that he would slip up and tell her about the baby. But she left a couple of days later and he said she didn't know anything about the pregnancy.

Jerry and I began to drift apart, seeing each other less and less, until I realized that I could actually date someone else. I met a young man at school who asked me out. He was tall, dark, and good-looking. We began to see each other quite often and I told Jerry what was happening. Jerry blew up and yelled at me, saying that he wanted me to move back in with him. Once he realized he was losing me, he wanted me back. I said no and we went our separate ways. I continued going to school and working, seeing Steve, the man from school, on a regular basis. We went camping and fishing. We visited his parents at their seaside vacation house on the coast of Oregon. We went deep sea fishing and crabbing. His parents liked me a lot, and they invited me over for dinner quite often. I spent holidays with them. We kept going down this track for about a year. And then, out of the blue, Steve said he wanted to break up. He chose to do this while we were out to dinner with his parents. A week before this incident, he had asked me to marry him.

I was devastated. He offered no explanation. I asked his mother what had happened and she told me that his father had done the same thing to her. She said Steve wanted to "look around" more before he committed to me. Why couldn't he explain that to me himself?

I was suffering over this break up, when my sister called me unexpectedly. She and Bob had moved back to Wyoming and were living in a small manufactured log home on an acre of land that Virginia and Don gave them. She told me that Virginia had been diagnosed with recurrent metastatic breast cancer and she wanted me to come home. I told Candy I would be there within a week. I packed up my things, fit them all into my Camaro and quit my job. I dropped out of school, left Oregon, and left Jerry for Wyoming in April of 1974 on another Big Adventure.

WELCOME TO WYOMING,
PART II

April 2024. Today is the first day of summer at the cabin. This morning I stood in the kitchen washing dishes and looking out my kitchen window at Table Mountain. Sixty years ago I was riding my horse up the Table Mountain trail with my mother. We had a picnic lunch in the saddlebags and we were looking for wild flowers. Shooting stars, pasque flowers, Indian paintbrush, deer moss, bluebells, lupine, larkspur. The list goes on. Mother's love of nature is something we had in common: I can name every wildflower in Wyoming. Thanks to my Aunt Shirley, I can name every Wyoming bird and then some. The gift of appreciating nature from two New England women that loved me is something I will always be grateful for.

Every path I followed over the past sixty years has led me back to my cabin in Wyoming. I wonder about Steve and what would have happened if we had married and lived in Oregon. What would have happened if I had stayed with Jerry? Instead, I took the road less traveled in every circumstance. Sometimes the choice was made for me by some outside force that I didn't understand until now. Candy and I shared a love of nature. She told me that if not for that, she would have gone off the deep end long ago. Now that I think of her, I remember going on bird walks and flower walks when she lived in Missouri. Whenever she called me, she would tell me about a new bird she saw at the feeder. I have no one left with which to share this bird and flower information. It saddens me. I miss all the Evans women who have died.

Despite the bad news about my mother's cancer returning, I was happy to be back in Wyoming again. I arrived in April during the worst snowstorm in decades. I barely made it up the Skull Creek Pass. My car and the roads were covered with icy slush and I drove about 30 miles per hour all the way from Billings to Cody. A fitting welcome for me. When I arrived in Wapiti at my mother's house, I staggered out of the car and ran up the steps. My mother actually hugged me. I couldn't recall a time when she had hugged me. She looked tired. Don was there, helping me bring in my suitcases, asking how the roads were. I was 24-years-old, and still I was barely able to be civil to him.

I don't know what I expected to happen with this visit. I thought I would go back to Oregon at some point. My mother seemed quite cheerful. We talked a lot and had tea and cookies. I offered to fix her hair. I thought I would spend the summer and then go back to school. She told me that she and Don were going to go back to New England in September, essentially a good-bye tour to see all her friends. She told me that Dr. Movius had given her a year, more or less, to live. The cancer was in her lungs. I realized going back to Oregon was not an option for me. I would stay until she no longer needed me.

Candy and Bob had moved back to Wyoming from New Hampshire a few years earlier. They brought Heather, their daughter, whom I had never met. She was eight years old at that time and was going to Wapiti School. My mother asked me to try and spend time with Heather because she (Heather) was in "a very difficult situation." I tried to get more details, but my mother just shrugged and said imagine if you were in her situation, living with Bob Livermore as your father.

I didn't really like children, but I tolerated Heather's company once in a while. She was a very shy child. Candy was working at the nursing home in Cody as an LPN. Bob apparently was not working, nor did he plan to. He spent a lot of time with his mother and brother, who lived about a mile down the road from my mother's house.

Yellowstone Park opened on May 10th every year. I drove my mother up to the Park around the end of June. We took a picnic lunch. The wild flowers were spectacular that year. We stopped at Yellowstone Lake where my mother had to use the outhouse. While she was in there, a huge bull buffalo ambled up to the Forest Service green structure and proceeded to rub his head on the outhouse door. I was sitting in the car waiting for my mother. I heard her hollering for me and I hollered back, telling her to stay in there until the buffalo moved on. We were laughing hysterically. Finally, he headed off down the foot trail and I rescued my mother from the outhouse.

I will always remember that day in Yellowstone with my mother. We were taking one day at a time, enjoying being together. I had never felt that with her before. She was always so busy and short-tempered. Don wasn't working so much and he took time off to be with Virginia. I was grateful to him for that. Right after Labor Day, Don and Virginia left for New England in their battered Ford pickup truck, pulling the camper trailer. My mother had many college friends who were still in touch. We had a lot of cousins and, of course, Auntie was still living in West Newton. I stayed behind to take care of the house, water her plants, and feed the two horses that were on the property. I took care of the chickens and fed Dingus the cat. I sat on the porch at night, looking up at Olive Fell's light. I wondered what would happen when Virginia died. We were all in a state of denial. I couldn't imagine that she would go down without a fight. I was tidying up her desk and typewriter table when I found an obituary she had written. I had to laugh. Only Virginia would write her own obituary, not trusting any of us to get it right. As I read the obituary, I realized how much she had accomplished in her life. I think her greatest accomplishment was bringing us all to Wyoming. She was a true pioneer. A strong, intelligent woman who was definitely not afraid to stand up for her beliefs.

I sat for a while staring out the window at Jim Mountain. A profound sadness overtook me as I thought of the fact that she would never know about her granddaughter born in Oregon on March 15, 1970.

She would never know the true reason why Don and I avoided each other. She would never know the truth about me. I had a long way to go before I would become aware of myself and my goals in life. It would be a long time before I could be at peace with myself and my life choices.

When Don and Virginia came back from New England, Virginia needed another round of chemotherapy. She was hospitalized in Billings for several weeks, extending through the Christmas holidays. When she came back home, we fixed up the guest room for her. She had a grand view of the mountains and the valley from her bedroom windows. Candy gave her pain injections as needed. I made her Jello and banana pudding. We watched the *Today Show* together. Barbara Walters and Hugh Downs. Her plan was to die at home. There was no real Hospice program at that time, but Candy and I took care of her. During the worst blizzard we had seen in years, my mother decided she needed to go to the hospital in Cody to die. The ambulance barely made it to pick her up and take her to the hospital. Don and I followed in two separate vehicles, using only the red tail lights of the ambulance as our guide through the storm.

Virginia died on February 9, 1975. Don had stayed late with her at the hospital, but she told him to go home. I had gone to a friend's house to get some sleep. She died alone on that cold snowy night, but that was what she wanted. We all gathered at the hospital the next morning. Virginia had donated her body to science so she was whisked off to the University Medical School in Denver. She was removed from our lives without a trace. The memorial service was held at Ballard Funeral Home with Reverend Buzzwell officiating. I remember it being a very nice service. We were all rather stunned by her absence. I don't remember anyone crying. She was the glue that held our family together and now she was gone.

And then there was the letter she wrote me when she was in Billings: January 9, 1975:

Dear Tina,

I never know from day to day whether I'll be able to communicate since there are so many things that can finish me off, so I'll write.

I worry so much now about you and how you're drifting that I get a stomachache. Staying with Betty so much isn't a good idea. You'll ruin that relationship as you do all of yours, by overdoing it.. You can't run forever from everything unpleasant.

Can you think back to when Don and I were married and you cried so when we left? Can you try to analyze why you were crying because I think it's important. Were you jealous? Did you feel Don had deserted you as everyone else always has seemed to do, or that I had?

I wish you would try to realize your potential and not be like all the rest who simply live on the surface because they can't bear to face reality.

I find it hard to face the end of my life knowing

I failed both you and Candy completely. At best you could learn from my mistakes and not turn away from everybody just because some little thing displeases you in them. Heather, for instance, needs you desperately. So does Don. He bristles at the sight of you now because you've rejected him so. Just staying and eating with him would help, and doing the dishes. You turn on your special charm for everyone, even the dogs, but not for him and he is extremely sensitive.

I'm sorry to be so blunt, but I have to say things now or never.

I doubt if I ever get home. You will have to have an auction and sell as much junk as possible after you and Candy take what you want. Edie is just sitting like a wolf waiting and she may likely win. So if I don't make it back be sure you and Candy take what you want.

Love, Mum

October 26, 2024

Dear Mum,

Another birthday remembrance. Another beautiful October day. I walked down by the river with the dogs this morning. The trees are still lovely, glowing orange and yellow with some light green leaves remaining. The river is low, but deep blue and clean.

As you know, I am writing a memoir of our lives, starting with our trip to Wyoming. Something we probably never would have done if Fred had lived. The courage it took for you to drag us to Wyoming always astounds me when I think of it. I see you now as a strong, independent woman. When I was younger, throughout all our trials and tribulations, I did not admire you. You were controlling and critical of me. You nagged everyone — Don, me, Candy. After you left us forever, I stumbled through life, not knowing what direction to take. I went with the flow. I took on whatever presented itself. I did not have any goals or ambitions.

It wasn't until I was dragged kicking and screaming by Halvorsen to New Mexico that I began to see my future. I worked hard and I endured Halvorsen's narcissism, bipolar personality, his addictions, and his tremendous self-absorption. I fought hard for my business and my freedom. I held onto my dream of returning to Wyoming and living in the cabin on Green Creek. And now here I am at age 74, a strong, independent woman, living my dream. You gave me Wyoming and I held onto it. My roots are here. The New England farm is far away. It must have hurt you terribly to give up that farm.

I sit on the porch of the cabin and admire Jim Mountain and the places we used to ride our horses and trail our cows. The Bradford Ranch, though short-lived, was an amazing experience for me. Being a Wyoming ranch kid implanted real values in me. Responsibility, dependability, honesty, and empathy. Now here I am on Green Creek, with the ranch house still down at the end of Green Creek. The barn is gone and most of the other out-buildings. The farm land has been turned into Copperleaf, a huge housing development which has attracted rich New Yorkers and Californians, driving up our property taxes. It is inevitable that the increasing population will soon ruin this valley.

I can still sit on my porch and admire the valley. The tall sagebrush hides us from the county road and all the neighbors. The creek runs quietly behind the cabin. The properties around us are empty. Eventually they will probably be sold, but for now we are alone, Greg and I, on our small patch of beautiful land, surrounded by my favorite mountains.

I have to tell you that when Candy died, I felt abandoned again. When you died, there was that same feeling of abandonment. You told me to "take care of Don" and I didn't feel that it was fair to put the whole thing on me. Everything pretty much went to hell after you died. Don met Carol and made the biggest mistake of his life, according to Aunt Dorothy. I was in New Mexico far away from all the mess. Now everyone is dead.

Still, I have that peaceful easy feeling I have been pursuing all my life. I have managed to quell the awfulizing most of the time. Worrying never actually helps anyone. I am taking my life one day at a time without nervously worrying about the future. What will be will be.

I look forward to our next conversation. Take care.

Love, Tina

THE AFTERLIFE

After my mother died, we all took a little time to gather ourselves together. After completing a few weeks of Emergency Medical Technician training, I took a job working in the Cody Hospital Emergency Room. I worked the 3-11 shift, so I got home very late. I managed to avoid seeing Don as much as I could. On weekends, I stayed in town with my friend, Betty. We did a lot of drinking and dancing at the Bronze Boot. I was simply living on the surface because I couldn't bear to face the reality of the situation, just as my mother said in her letter. When I did go home, Don was usually sleeping, and by the time I got up the next day, he was already off working.

One night I got home particularly late after a lot of drinking. I went to bed immediately and was sleeping very soundly when I felt the pressure of someone sitting on the end of the bed. I thought someone was touching my leg through the covers. I sat up and saw Don sitting there, quietly rubbing my leg. "I miss your mother," he said. I pulled my legs up and hugged them tightly. "I miss her, too," I said. We sat there quietly not saying anything, and then he sighed and left the room. The old

fear began rising in the pit of my stomach. I was twenty-
four years old and still had the terrifying feeling of dread
I had when I was fourteen. I knew I had to get out of
that house. The following weekend I was back at the
Bronze Boot with some girlfriends from work when a
young man named Mark came over to our table and sat
down by me. He said he remembered me when we were
students together at Wapiti School. It all came back to
me. He and his family owned Holm Lodge which was
a local dude ranch. We rode the school bus together. He
said he had always had a crush on me.

We talked for several hours, sharing a few drinks
and ordering food. During this time, he cleared his
throat and said that he had a proposition for me. I was
intrigued. He said that he had taken a job as caretaker of
a large property owned by rich people from New York.
The house was on the Four-Bear Ranch, which was Olive
Fell's property. She had sold a portion of her property
to Bill and Dusty Weiss, who built a huge house there,
and they were only there a few times in the summertime.
He asked me if I would like to come be a caretaker with
him. Without hesitation I said I would love to. This was
my way out of the Don situation. We made plans to meet
the next day to organize our move to the Weiss house.

Mark Spragg was an honorable young man. He
mistakenly thought that Don was my father and, as such,
he was obligated to explain to Don about our moving
in together and ask his permission to do so. Mark did
this without talking to me. I was a little taken aback,
but apparently Don approved and told Mark that he
gave his permission. I moved up to the Weiss house with

Mark, leaving a lot of my possessions in the basement of Don's house. I never really thought of it as Don's house, and since my mother had sold her New Hampshire farm in order to build the house, I always thought of it as her house.

Mark and I moved into the caretaker's apartment on the first floor of the 7500 square foot mansion nestled under the east rim of Jim Mountain. The house was gorgeous inside and out. No expense had been spared with the use of lichen-covered rock and timber. Fred Garlow, the property manager and relative of Buffalo Bill Cody, showed us around the property and explained our duties. I was to clean the enormous house and put fresh sheets and towels in the bedrooms and bathrooms. Mark's job was to keep an eye on the plumbing and electricity, making sure that nothing was amiss. He had access to a four-wheel drive pickup with a snowplow on the front. During the winter, we were to keep the thermostat set at 60, but could turn up the heat accordingly if outside temperatures reached 20 below or more. We had a separate thermostat for our apartment.

When I look back at all the events in my life, I see a familiar pattern. Every time I needed rescuing, someone or something presented itself as a way out of a situation or as an escape hatch. Sometimes I just needed help, but there it was standing in the wings, ready to give me a hand. In my desperate need to leave Don, Mark stepped in and provided a way out. It took me a long time to accept the fact that everything always works out. No amount of worrying or anxiety is necessary for me. There is always a way to fix something or get something

I need. Everything happens for a reason has become my life mantra. My Aunt Shirley said there were angels looking out for us all the time. One time when she was shopping in downtown Boston, she started to step off the curb right in front of an oncoming bus. She told me that she felt two firm hands on her shoulders and she was jerked back up onto the sidewalk. When she turned around, there was no one there. Similar things happened to her throughout her life.

When Mark asked me to caretake the Weiss house with him, I didn't hesitate. I liked Mark but I didn't really know him very well. He was younger than me and we didn't have the same friends or interests. He was a good-looking young man with reddish brown hair. He wasn't tall, maybe 5' 8" or so, and he was a little full of himself, but he had a good sense of humor. He always wore jeans and cowboy boots. He was clean and neat and tidy. After a year of care-taking, Mark asked me to marry him. I agreed and we were married in the original Episcopal church in Cody. Candy, Bob, Heather and Don attended

We got along fine in the beginning but after a few months, he started to be more critical. I liked his mother, Phyllis, but she was controlling as well. She bought clothes for me and insisted that I wear them. They were not always things I would have chosen. She contradicted almost everything I said. She told me what to do and how to act. I felt smothered.

Jesse Spragg, Mark's father, was an alcoholic. He and Phyllis ran Holm Lodge for a while, but sold it after a few years. Jesse went into real estate and did quite well. He was actually a functional alcoholic. He didn't start drinking until after work. He was a surly, angry man when he was drinking. With Jesse as an example, Mark became surly and angry when he was drinking. We were staying at Phyllis's house one weekend. Mark went into town to play pool and drink with his friend, Ted Feeley. Phyllis and I played cards and fixed ourselves dinner. I went to bed around 9:00 p.m. Mark came home around 1:00 a.m., extremely drunk and staggering. He came into the bedroom where I was sleeping and turned on the light. He proceeded to yell at me and threatened me. I asked him what in the hell was wrong with him. In answer to that, he grabbed me by the shoulders and shoved me up against the bedroom wall. He then turned around and passed out on the bed. I waited a few minutes to make sure he was out and then grabbed my coat and purse and very quietly left the house. Mark had left his old Scout running, so I very carefully eased it out of the driveway and drove back up to the Weiss house. I was scared and on the verge of crying. I took the phone off the hook and sat on the couch, wondering what to do. I didn't get much sleep that night. I assumed when he sobered up he would apologize, but I didn't think I would accept an apology. I left the phone off the hook the next day until about 5:00 pm. When I put it back on the hook, it rang immediately. I didn't answer it. This went on all evening. Finally, I answered the phone. It was Phyllis. She said don't you think you are carrying this a little too far? I didn't think so, given the fact that Mark had physically shoved me in a drunken rage.

However, I was willing to talk to him. I drove down

to the Spragg house and he was there waiting with a large bunch of flowers and a heart-felt apology. He told me he was giving up alcohol and I believed him. In fact, during the rest of our time together, he did not drink.

We met Bill and Dusty that fall shortly after we moved in. Dusty was a delightful woman. She was kind and thoughtful. They were very fond of Mark and me and treated us like family. When they were there by themselves, Dusty would summon us for dinner and drinks. She poured us Dom Perignon in chilled silver chalices. Bill was usually in his cups after dinner and would excuse himself and go to bed. Dusty, Mark and I would stay up playing cards and board games. One evening Dusty retrieved a Ouija board from her cupboard and we set that up and tried it out. Mark went first and received positive messages about his writing. Dusty received messages from her mother. We were amused and laughing. When I placed my fingers on the planchette, it began to move very fast, spelling out "We are Siva Welcome to our world." Over and over again it spelled out "We are Siva." We began to be a little nervous so we put the board away and said goodnight.

Several days later I was sitting in the kitchen of our apartment making a grocery list as I was going into town to run errands. I had written a few things on the list and was thinking, with the pen poised in my hand. All of a sudden my hand began to move and the pen was lowered to the list. I began to write "We are Siva. We have come to you to help you." My hand was moving on its own with no help from me. The writing, therefore, was very scribbled but legible. I kept writing. "We are a group of people who are here to help you." I was freaking out. I stopped writing and got up from the table. Mark was down at his mother's house. I wondered what to do, but I stayed calm. I had heard of automatic writing in my travels through psychology books and spiritualism studies. This seemed like automatic writing.

I drove to town and went to the library. I found several books on "psychography" and the art of automatic writing. The means to access your soul by using an unconscious method. I was impressed. I checked out two of the books. I finished my grocery shopping and drove home.

Mark was home by then and I explained what had happened. He was open-minded about spiritualism and was fascinated by my explanation. He asked me to try to write with him in the room. I did and I was able to access my "spirits" and continue with the automatic writing. Mark asked me questions to ask the spirits and we spent all afternoon engaged in this activity until I was really tired out and had to stop.

I continued automatic writing throughout the time that Mark and I were caretakers at the Weiss house. The messages from Siva were always positive and helpful. However, I began to think I was the one doing the writing and that maybe I was mentally unbalanced. I stopped writing for a while, but then returned to it, thinking that I should pursue it until I no longer needed it. I filled hundreds of yellow legal pads, carefully dating them and storing them in boxes. I read everything I could find on automatic writing and spiritualism. I looked up Siva and found that Siva or Shiva is the supreme being of

Hinduism. Siva is God or Allah. When I was contacting Siva, I was always reminded that Siva was what the group of spirits called themselves. So I decided that I wasn't really in touch with God himself.

At the beginning of our second year of care-taking, Bill and Dusty built a small, two bedroom caretaker's house about a quarter of a mile south of the big house. We moved into that house in September of 1977. The house was much larger than our little apartment and we had all the amenities: dishwasher, washer and dryer, a full finished basement, hardwood floors. We were happy with the new house and we looked forward to another winter in a more comfortable situation.

I met Steve Halvorsen (most of his friends and family just called him Halvorsen) for the first time in the fall of 1977. He had been living in Iowa to be closer to his three-year-old daughter and had just returned to Wyoming to live with his father at the cabin on Green Creek. Mark befriended Halvorsen when they were attending the University of Wyoming and had several of Steve's paintings. When I commented on the paintings, Mark teased me and told me that if I ever met Halvorsen I would run away with him, but Mark invited him to dinner anyway. Mark and I had just moved into the caretaker's house. I remember standing at the sink looking out at the road wondering if the man called Halvorsen would be able to negotiate the winding dirt road with four cattle guards, turn left instead of right, and cross the left fork of the creek. Mark saw him first and went outside to open the gate into our driveway.

I glanced out the kitchen window and saw a bright

orange Karmann Ghia pull up. Halvorsen stepped out, wearing a wool Mexican serape and a gray felt fedora with a hawk feather hanging off the back. A tall man with a Tom Selleck mustache, long golden-brown hair, Levis, boots, and sparkling white teeth. I went into the bathroom and sat on the edge of the tub. My face was flushed and I had chest tightness. Never had I seen such a magnificent beast. I heard Mark bringing him into the house, talking, laughing. I splashed cold water on my face and went out into the living room. He was a charmer and I liked him immediately. Dinner went well with wine and university stories. We laughed hysterically. He left quite late. Mark and I cleaned up and chatted. I went to bed trying to shake off the magic dust Halvorsen had scattered around the room. An artist, photographer, jack of all trades, master of them all. A Renaissance man, capable of everything. How long had I looked for someone like that and given up ever finding anyone? I married Mark the writer because we were friends who liked each other and I was tired of holding out for romance. We saw a lot of Halvorsen that fall. Dinners, art openings, parties, functions. He was always there flashing that bright perfect smile, telling amazing stories and making us laugh. He was the star of the show, the leading man, dazzling us all and blinding many of us.

Over the ensuing winter Halvorsen lured me away from Mark with the premise that we were meant to be together. Fate had thrown us together and you couldn't ignore fate. Halvorsen told Mark that we had fallen in love and I was leaving Mark and the mountain to begin a new life with him. The damage was done. Gossip ran rampant throughout the valley. I divorced Mark, the writer, and married Halvorsen, the artist.

Steve rented a house from Jim Bama for $400 a month. The house was the original structure on the Dunn Creek property in which Jim and Lynn Bama lived when they first came to Wyoming. They subsequently built a house for themselves about a quarter of a mile north of the old house. Steve told me we would be living there and that he was going to do darkroom work for Jim, a well-known Western artist who utilized black and white photography as studies for his oil paintings. Jim was famous for his portraits of Native Americans and aging Wyoming ranchers.

Halvorsen worked for a short while for *Wyoming News Magazine* as an art director. His bipolar high lasted for about four years, during which time he moved the house to a two-acre Green Creek property, renovated it, built an exquisite artist studio, borrowed money from the bank at an alarming rate, and drove our expenses up to the point where we couldn't pay the mortgage.

We moved from the valley to Albuquerque, New Mexico in 1981. Halvorsen decided we needed to be near Santa Fe where the art market was fresh. We were on the brink of monetary disaster. With bankruptcy gnawing at our heels, we put our house on the market, loaded a U-Haul and made the trek to New Mexico. I was dragged, mentally kicking and screaming, to a place in the desert that held no meaning for me. We arrived during a windstorm, with tumbleweed the size of small cars hitting the truck as we drove through the blowing sand.

Uprooted and frightened, we found a house to rent, unloaded our belongings and tried to settle in. I worked for a dermatologist as a medical assistant and did medical transcription for several other doctors. Halvorsen declared he was going to "do his own work" and it became evident that I would have to pay the bills. Anyone with any knowledge of bipolar disease will understand that paying the bills was a gargantuan task.

Halvorsen had problems directing the horrendous energy of a bipolar high. He was always preparing to work. First, he cleaned the studio from top to bottom, even if it had been done the week before. He inventoried his supplies. He rearranged the furniture. He smoked his pipe and contemplated the situation. At this point he started to complain that he didn't have the right equipment. His space was too small or the light wasn't right. A plan would emerge changing his whole perspective on working. A new easel or new brushes from England. He absolutely had to have these things before he could possibly entertain the thought of beginning a new project. He brought out the calculator and sat me down to explain the cost and how we were going to pay for all these things he needed. If I raised a voice of reason, he would go ahead with his plan despite my objections. He pitched his plans to his father and borrowed money from him. He talked someone into a commission and obtained a down payment for a painting.

He had a closet full of half finished commissions. If anyone inquired as to when their painting would be done, he was insulted. He did finish a few of them.

The others sat in the closet for years, making their way to the dump when I cleaned out his belongings. I was embarrassed by his dishonesty. I'm still embarrassed.

The scope of his mental illness was complicated and twisted. He had a way of making everyone think they were the crazy ones. Yet, when he did complete a project, a painting or a series of etchings, his work was spectacular. This was the reason I held on so long. I believed in him and his talent. I wanted him to be successful, to shine. I didn't understand the bipolar element of his personality nor did he. He brought himself to the brink of success many times and then would destroy himself somehow. Financially, usually. He had grandiose ideas beyond his ability to carry them out. He was the handsome rock star who overwhelmed everyone with whom he came in contact. I was the drab little housewife who trotted along behind him picking up the debris.

Halvorsen did not believe in his own talent. He copied his work, albeit it was a stunning copy. His work did not come from him, from his heart. It was dishonest work, done well, carried out well beyond what the original artist could do. He went through art magazines looking for his style. He would clip paintings, ones he thought were him, and pin them on a cork board in his studio. He believed they were his paintings. He tried them out on himself. No amount of talking with friends or other artists could convince him that he should find his own way, his own work. He always wanted what other people had but he didn't want to put in the time it took to get there.

Halvorsen's whirling dervish lifestyle finally did me in. In the beginning, he mesmerized women. He gave them what they wanted — romance. He was the king of romance. The knight on the white horse, banners flying, armor shining, sword drawn. Freeing them from the tower, galloping away with the maiden behind him on the horse, riding into the sunset with the promise of happiness. As long as they could write him a check, he kept them. When the money ran out, he was gone.

I remember him standing in front of the bathroom mirror, grooming himself like a neurotic Amazon parrot. Applying Coppertone bronzing cream to his face, combing his great lion's mane of hair, checking for lines around his eyes. When I first met him, he had a mustache that took a lot of grooming as well. He looked like he belonged in a cowboy movie. The felt hat with the hawk feather hanging down the back. The way he flipped his hair, like a woman. He could have been a big movie star with the teeth and the hair and the 6 foot 4 inch body. He could have been so much. Instead, he struggled with mental illness and addiction, bipolar disorder with manic highs lasting for years. Countless affairs with attractive women.

I felt like such a fool. I hung on longer than most with Steve. I believed in him. I wanted him to succeed. I did everything to keep the fairy tale alive, but he didn't cooperate. I hung on through bankruptcy, bipolar lows, insane money-making schemes, knowing most of the time how wrong he was, but never telling him. I supported him through every manic phase of his life, his spending sprees, when he drank too much and embarrassed me. I forgave him. I loved him. In the end, I drove him away to save my own life. He had taken my soul as well as my money. He sucked every ounce of energy out of me until I was empty. I had no idea who I was. I had to make it stop. At that point, I suggested that he move back to Wyoming and live in the cabin on Green Creek that we had purchased from his father. We divorced but kept joint custody of the cabin. I sent him money and paid the mortgage and the property taxes. Anything to have some peace and quiet and start to save my own life. It took me years to clean up the financial earthquake rubble he left behind.

Once Halvorsen left for Wyoming, my medical transcription business started to take off. I employed ten subcontractors who worked out of their homes. I set up software to connect all of us to a large oncology contract with digital call-in devices instead of tapes. I had countless other contracts with smaller medical practices. With Halvorsen gone, I began making a lot of money. For twenty-five years I stayed in Albuquerque running my business and planning for retirement. I was careful to keep my financial successes a secret from Steve. When my Aunt Shirley died in 2001, she left me $60,000. I very carefully set up a retirement fund with this money, along with monthly withdrawals from my checking account. Steve asked me if Auntie had left me any money. I told him there was no inheritance.

Over the years Halvorsen and I kept in contact. Whenever he had a new woman in his life there were long silences. No phone calls, no frantic ploys for money. However, no one could stand to live with him for long and the affairs did not last. He always picked women who were already entangled in a relationship and tried to steal them away as he had done with me when we first met. His drinking got worse and he became angrier, his hypochondria increased and he took more pills. He went into rehab and came out ready to go back to drinking. There were agonizing phone calls and emergency room visits, hospitalizations, and drama. Halvorsen had fallen from grace for the last time that September and there was nothing to be done. He killed himself on the porch of the cabin, finally giving me the way to come home. He took Wyoming away from me, but with that single act of pulling the trigger on the shotgun, he gave it back to me.

THE AFTERMATH

I saw Don for the last time in the grocery store. He told me that he was dating a woman he met through the personal ads in the paper. I had just left Mark for Halvorsen and Don asked what had happened. I just shrugged without answering him. I wished him good luck with his dating and left the store. Several weeks later he called me and told me he was getting married. He asked me to come to the house and help him with Virginia's stuff. He told me to take anything I wanted.

Candy and I spent about a week going through everything. His fiancée, Carole, stopped by and introduced herself. She was quite a bit younger than Don. She began going through all the rooms, muttering that she was living with a ghost. Candy and I exchanged glances and went on with our sorting and cleaning. Ironically, Carole was a journalist who wrote a column for the *Cody Enterprise*. As it turned out, after they were married Carole made Don change his will. Carole had a daughter and a son. She wanted Don to adopt them, but he refused. Instead she made him change the will, which originally had me as the beneficiary. My name was erased and she and her children were added. In addition to changing the will, Carole called Candy and me and told us we were no longer welcome there.

After the wedding it was discovered that Carole was pregnant and she gave birth to a son. Dorothy told me years later that Don was so proud of his son, but Carole wouldn't let him spend much time with the boy. By that time I was living in Albuquerque with Steve and heard things through the grapevine, mostly from our friend, Katy Roes. Candy, Heather and Bob had moved to Missouri shortly before Steve and I moved to New Mexico. One day Candy called me and related to me the fact that Don had sexually abused Heather. Candy asked me if I thought this was true because Heather was known to be a pathological liar. I told Candy I was sure it was true and I told her what had happened to me. Candy proceeded to write Don a letter accusing him of exposing Heather to filth and sexual abuse. She said no matter what the statute of limitations was, she would pursue charges. She sent me a copy of the letter. She sent copies to Auntie and our cousin Caroline.

A few weeks later I was sitting at my new Tandy-1000 computer transcribing tapes when the phone rang. It was Katy Roes. She told me that Don had died in a backhoe accident. She said the seat was all twisted and the bolts had been removed. She told me that the tracks had run over his head. The obituary stated that it was an accident. The rest of us knew that it was a suicide and that, essentially, Candy had killed Don. When Katy called and told me about Don, I was stunned. After we hung up, I cried uncontrollably. When I heard about what he did to Heather, I had nightmares about killing him. The thought never left my mind, and now the deed was done. The next day there was a message on my answering machine from Carole telling me that neither Candy nor I were to come to the funeral. Little did she know that neither of us wanted to go.

I talked to Heather about Don. She told me that when I left for the Weiss house with Mark, Don focused his attention on her. For two years he sexually molested her, but then stopped when he met Carole and got married. It had not occurred to me that he would molest anyone else. I thought the incident with me was the only one. I thought it was my fault and my problem to handle by myself. Obviously, I was wrong.

TAMY

Over the years on her birthday, I thought about my daughter. I thought about her at other times, mostly at night when I couldn't sleep. But on her birthday, I wondered what she was doing and what she looked like. When I was living in Albuquerque I heard from Katy Roes quite often.

She told me that she had been adopted as a baby. Her parents told her the truth about her adoption, but Katy had no interest in looking for her biological mother or father at that time. However, when she was older and had children of her own, she decided to look for biological relatives. She told me about a company called International Soundex where she had registered with her information in case anyone was looking for her. She gave me the information and I registered with them, thinking that if anyone was ever looking for me, they would have the means to find me.

I was still living with Steve and I told him about my daughter and the information Katy had given me. Typically, Steve said, "Can't you just let it go?" I was offended by his attitude, as usual. And I thought to myself, *no, I can't just let it go.*

In 1994 Steve and I divorced after I discovered yet another affair he was having while he was living at the cabin. For several years I continued updating my registration with International Soundex. I kept my same phone number and address in case she was looking. I went on with my life, always with the thought that I might find her.

It was December 24, 1997. I was in the shower getting ready for Christmas Eve dinner with friends. The phone rang and I let voice mail pick it up. In the flurry of dressing and wrapping packages, I forgot the call, but then I checked it. There was a message from Susan Braun of International Soundex. She gave me her home number. She said she had a great Christmas gift from them to me. Immediately I knew what it was. I sat at my round oak table and wept. I was thrilled and scared to death at the same time. I paced around the house for about 20 minutes, and then I made the call. Yes, Susan said, they had matched me up with my daughter. Her name was Tamy (one M and a Y). She lived in Orem, Utah, eight hundred miles from Albuquerque. She was looking for me. Susan gave me the phone number. "She wants to talk to you," she said. I was crying so hard I could barely croak out words. I wrote the number down and thanked Susan. I paced frantically again. Finally, I dialed the number. A familiar-sounding voice answered the phone. "Tamy," I said, "I'm your mother."

After we stopped crying, we finally began to talk. Tamy told me that she had always lived in Utah. She had not been told of her adoption. In August 1997 she received a letter from her niece and in the letter her niece replied to something Tammy had said about feeling estranged from her family. "It must be because you were adopted," she wrote. This was the first Tamy had heard of her adoption. She was understandably shocked. It took her a few weeks to digest the information.

She talked to her older sister who confirmed that Tamy was adopted as a baby. Their mother had just lost a baby and wanted to adopt one to replace the one who had died. Tamy was angry and confused. She had always felt that she didn't fit in with the family. She was the odd one out, the rebel in a family of Mormons. Her adoptive mother had banned her from the house after Tamy graduated from high school because she didn't approve of Tamy's lifestyle and friends. She had not talked to her adoptive parents for years. Her older sister suggested that Tamy register with International Soundex, which she did. On December 24, 1997 we were reunited.

She asked if she could call me Mom and I said of course you can. She did ask me why I gave her up, and I told her the reasons I had at the time. She asked me if I had named her, but I said I hadn't, though I did think about what she might have been named. We talked for a long time, but finally had to hang up because we were exhausted. She told me she would call me the next day.

Tamy and I talked on the phone for a couple of months. It was hard to get used to the fact that we were family. She asked me a lot of questions about the past and my family. I answered them all honestly. She asked about her father. I knew he was still in Oregon, so I called him and told him about Tamy. He cried and told me this was between Tamy and me. He said he felt like he was abandoning her all over again. Tamy sent him pictures and her address and told him that whatever he wanted to do was fine with her. I called my sister and my Aunt Shirley shortly after the Christmas eve phone call. They were both thrilled and touched by the story. A true Christmas miracle, they said.

Tamy told me that she felt her whole life so far had been a lie. She sent me pictures, one where she was five years old. She looked just like me at that age. She sent current pictures and there was a lovely 27-year-old young woman with my family resemblance. She looked like Granny and Virginia. She had Jerry's nose and my eyes. She had beautiful porcelain skin inherited from Jerry's Danish mother.

We talked about getting together and she was a little reluctant at first. We were scared, I think, to actually see each other in person. However, she agreed and in February I sent her a plane ticket. She told me she had never been on an airplane. When she stepped off the plane, I knew her. We were nervous and tense on the drive to my house, but after we started cooking dinner together, we loosened up. Tamy said she was vegetarian, so we worked around that and made pasta with spicy shrimp and a salad.

In the years since, we have spent a lot of time together. We traveled to England and Scotland in 2001. We spent Christmases together in Albuquerque. When Greg and I moved to Wyoming, she came to the cabin for a week every summer and we explored Yellowstone, Cooke City and Red Lodge. The more time we spent together, I could sense some of her anger was lessening.

She was angry with everybody. I was sad about the fact that she hadn't gone to college. She had no interest in anything. She had a flat affect and she said she hated people. She didn't know how to interact with people on a friendly, polite basis.

Tamy was 27 years old when we met. I was 47 years old. I think back on that first meeting and realize that we both have changed considerably. We are more at ease with each other. She seems happier. She met all my family; Candy, Caroline, and Auntie, although Auntie was teetering on the edge of Alzheimer's at the time. She did have enough of her mind left to change her will to include Tamy. Now I am 75 and she is 55. It seems to us both that we have known each other a very long time.

THE ENDING

We have been hammered over the past two months with winter storm watches, arctic blasts and winter snow advisories. Today, as I sit with my coffee looking out at Jim Mountain covered with tons of snow, I realize that I still want to be here. Greg has shoveled snow and hauled wood in 40-below weather. His state of mind is not as serene as mine. In fact, yesterday he said cabin fever was setting in so he drove to town for groceries and was gone for three hours. I have been known to do the same thing. I usually go to the library to kill some time. In fact, I was doing just that about six years ago when I spotted a familiar face. Mark Spragg was ordering lunch from the sandwich shop in the library. He sat down at the table next to mine. We looked at each other. "Hey, Mark." I said. Recognition spread across his face. "Tina!" he said.

We hugged and he sat at my table with his sandwich. We caught up while we ate our lunches. The same old Mark sat across from me, balding reddish-brown hair, a little heavier in the middle. But still the same neat and tidy Mark I remembered so well. I told him about a book I had just self-published. He told me about his latest book and his last screenplay. I told him about the memoir and how hard I was struggling with all the information running through my head. He told me he was sorry that he wasn't a better husband to me, but blamed his father for his shortcomings. I told him not to worry about it. He told me he was living in Red Lodge, Montana with his wife, Virginia. I told him I was living at the cabin on Green Creek with Greg and our two dogs. He gave me his address so I could send him my book and we went our separate ways.

I was happy to see Mark. I take great comfort in the fact that he is happily married and living the writing life in Red Lodge. We have traveled long and dusty roads, only to come back to our roots in the Absaroka mountains. As I review all the main events in my past lives, I find everything that has happened or changed was meant to be. One experience led to another.

Important people in my life have come and gone. And all roads led me back to the cabin on Green Creek.

EPILOGUE

Last night the rains came and took the last of the cottonwood leaves. The wind came and blew the rain and later snow and yellow leaves. This morning there is fresh powdered snow on Ptarmigan and Jim. Strands of wispy fog float over the river. Two buck deer feed on the lawn. Here at the cabin on Green Creek, my husband and I are ready for winter. Firewood is stacked shoulder-high on the porch. The two old dogs sleep on their round L.L. Bean dog beds near the warmth of the fire. It is late October in Wyoming.

Three weeks ago the cottonwood and aspen trees were in full color, enhanced by the slanting fall sun. I took the dogs for a long walk on the Clock Tower Creek trail. It is an easy horse trail and the dogs love to go. The beauty of the orange and gold leaves, along with purple asters and red chokecherry leaves, took my breath away. The cloudless October sky was painfully blue. The air was clean and crisp. The dogs drank from the creek. I stood at the end of our trail and breathed in the dank mossy smell of the water. We made our way slowly back to the car, reluctant to leave that wonderful place on such a day.

Now the leaves are off the trees and lying on my lawn, ready to be raked. The wind will help us in that regard, but there are always some stragglers. There is a certain sadness lingering with me at this time of year. It is too cold to sit on the porch in the evenings. The wind howls around the eaves. But I feel safe and secure in my log cabin with a low fire burning in the fireplace insert. A pot of homemade chili simmers on the old porcelain wood stove in the kitchen. A pile of new novels is stacked by my overstuffed chair. Winter hibernation has begun.

Looking out over the valley from my reading chair, I remembered the first time I saw my cabin. I met Harold Halvorsen back in the summer of 1977. He was a short, stocky Norwegian man, who built this cabin on Green Creek, just outside of Cody, half-way up the road to Yellowstone Park. The cabin was set back from the road in a nest of cottonwood trees, close to the creek.

Originally from Iowa, Harold and his wife, Eloise, planned to retire here when Harold's job as band director for Powell High School played out. Eloise, however, died of cancer before that could happen. Harold worked a few extra years, and then retired to the cabin by himself. He never remarried. He traveled to Spain and other parts of Europe. He busied himself with cabin chores, and he cross-country skied in the wintertime. He drank brandy and played cards with his neighbors. He sat on the porch and read Louis L'amour novels.

On Sunday mornings during the summertime, Harold fired up an old wood stove he had outside by the creek. He made sourdough pancakes for anyone who wished to show up. I was seeing his son, Steve, at the time and we drove to the cabin on a Sunday morning for the best pancakes in the world, according to Steve. Harold waved his spatula in greeting to us and told us to haul up a chair on the porch. He presented me with a plate of sourdough pancakes and a pitcher of homemade chokecherry syrup. To this day I believe this to be the best breakfast I have ever had or will ever hope to have in my lifetime.

Sitting on the porch that Sunday morning, eating pancakes and looking out over the valley at Jim Mountain, I had a strange feeling of having been here before. I had grown up in Wapiti Valley. There were many times in my childhood when I had ridden my horse right by this spot before there was a cabin here. The Halvorsens bought the land in 1964 and built the cabin over a period of years, ending in 1968. That was the year I graduated from high school. Now here I was back in the valley, on this porch, looking out at the places I knew well. Harold must have sensed it, as he leaned over to me while everyone else was busy eating pancakes. "It's good to come home, don't you think?" he said. I was near tears and just nodded my head. He patted my shoulder and went back to cooking.

Harold was a kind man, but because he was a Virgo, he was detached. He had his own life and he lived it the way he wanted. He was self-centered, but in a good way. Steve and I married in 1978, and we saw a lot of Harold. We moved into a house just a few miles down the road from the cabin. We drove our Ford trucks up on Rattlesnake Mountain and cut wood for the winter.

We went skiing together in the winter and fishing in the summer. We camped up on the Clark's Fork and we spent a lot of time sitting on the porch at the cabin. Steve and I took care of the cabin when Harold went on his European trips. We had Halvorsen family reunions at the cabin. We had fish-fries, pancake cookouts, picnics by the creek, hikes up the Table Mountain trail.

Life was good on Green Creek, and Harold was happily enjoying his retirement.

Harold's lawn was his pride and joy. He irrigated the lawn by pumping water from the creek. He spent a lot of time mowing, trimming, weeding, and watering. I was working at the emergency room in town while Steve was busy being an artist. One day Harold came sauntering into the emergency room and asked if we could talk. We sat down for coffee in the cafeteria, and he began to tell me that he was having chest pains when he mowed the lawn. Sometimes he didn't have pain, just an overwhelming fatigue and some shortness of breath. Alarmed, I asked him to talk to the ER doctor, and he agreed, so we signed him up. As it turned out, Harold was having angina, and when he was worked up by the internist, he was found to have 90% blockage in almost all his arteries. He underwent immediate surgery in Billings, a quadruple by-pass. He sailed through this and came home to the cabin to recover. We helped him with the lawn and his chores, but after about six weeks, he was up doing everything he always did. However, he was getting older, and he had to admit that he should slow down a little bit. It became too much for him to chop wood and do heavy yard work. At the end of the summer, Harold decided to shut the cabin down for the winter and spend his time traveling in the Southwest. He bought a Scamp travel trailer and off he went, happy to be a snowbird spending his winters in Arizona with all the other elderly people. Steve and I moved to New Mexico in 1982. Harold visited us frequently, parking his Scamp in our back yard. He was happy with his nomadic lifestyle, but he missed his cabin on Green Creek.

The beginning of the end came for Harold on a windy spring day in New Mexico. Harold packed up his travel trailer, loaded up the dog, and said good-bye to Steve and me as he headed out for a campground south of Socorro, New Mexico. Several hours later, the phone call arrived from a state trooper who asked if we knew a Harold Halvorsen. A heavy gust of wind had caused him to lose control and topple his trailer and Ford Ranger, rolling them several times in the barren sage-covered plains of southern New Mexico. The dog had been thrown clear and skulked off in the sage, and it took several hours to coax him back. Harold, it seems, had been lucky. A broken collarbone and lots of bruises. For this 78-year-old man, traveling by himself and camping out in remote areas, everything changed on this blustery spring day. He had to come to terms with the fact that he couldn't do this anymore. With his trailer and vehicle totaled, Harold found an apartment in a retirement community near our house in Albuquerque. He spent most of his time sitting in a lawn chair reading a book. The dog came to live with us. Harold's carefree camping life was no more. He sold his cabin to Steve and me. He felt useless and old. He complained a lot and watched TV for hours on end. He had to rely on public transportation. I drove him around whenever possible, but I worked many hours a week. His three daughters lived thousands of miles away, and they couldn't convince him to come stay with them. Steve went back up to Wyoming to live for the summer in the cabin on Green Creek. Harold was stuck in a big city he didn't like, with a busy daughter-in-law whom he did like, but he pined. He became weaker and more frail. He lost weight. He had more aches and pains. His life was running out.

Steve and I split up shortly after Harold's accident. Steve decided to stay in Wyoming and live in the Halvorsen cabin. We retained joint custody of the cabin during the divorce. I convinced Harold to move back to Cody in assisted living so he could be close to Steve and he could visit the cabin once in a while. Two years later Harold developed pancreatic cancer and some kind of leukemia-like blood disorder. He refused chemotherapy. I made the trip to Wyoming in early summer to say good-bye to him. He was in the hospice unit at the hospital. I sat by his bedside and talked to him for a while. I leaned close to hear him whisper, "Don't let Steve have the cabin. It belongs to you. Take good care of it." Two days later he died.

I wasn't always very patient with Harold in the later years because I was very busy working and he required a lot of care. He couldn't drive and he had nothing that interested him. He walked into the house any time of the day and sat watching TV while I tried to work. He wanted to visit with me and I was sometimes very abrupt with him. Steve took advantage of Harold, used his credit cards without his knowledge, and in the end took all of the estate for himself, though there wasn't much, but it was supposed to be divided up among all the children. I did love Harold. I will always remember him living at the cabin on Green Creek, cooking sourdough pancakes on his old wood stove and serving them up with his homemade chokecherry syrup.

Steve committed suicide in 2003, thus leaving me as the sole owner of the cabin. I think about Harold quite a bit these days. I think how lucky I am to have his cabin. I hope he can see me here. I hope he knows how much I love this place. The Norwegian high school band director who found a magical spot of land and built this sturdy log cabin. I will be forever grateful to Harold Halvorsen for my cabin on Green Creek.

CHRISTINA WRAY